YEAR ONE
SPRING

Y0-ABB-369

An Inspiring Two-Year Journey Through The Bible
From The Library Of
MARY McCORKLE

Old Testament Devotional Commentary
NIZAR & ELLEN SHAHEEN

New Testament Devotional Commentary
JIM & KATHY CANTELON

Inspirational "Prayer For Today" portions
DAVID & NORMA-JEAN MAINSE

A ministry of Crossroads Christian Communications Inc.

In Canada:
Crossroads Christian
Communications Inc.
100 Huntley Street
Toronto, Ontario
M4Y 2L1

Bus: (416) 961-8001

In the USA:
Crossroads Christian
Communications Inc.
Box 486
Niagara Falls, NY
14302

Prayer: (416) 961-1500

ISBN 0-921702-12-4
Copyright 1989 ©CROSSROADS CHRISTIAN COMMUNICATIONS INC.

Published by **CROSSROADS CHRISTIAN COMMUNICATIONS INC.**
100 Huntley Street, Toronto, Ontario, Canada M4Y 2L1

Printed in Canada
Harmony Printing Limited
123 Eastside Drive, Toronto, Ontario, Canada M8Z 5S5

Scripture quotations are from the New King James Version and are used with permission of Thomas Nelson Publishers. Copyright ©1979, 1980, 1982.

Cover photo by D. Muench/Miller Comstock

Holy Land photos courtesy of the Israel Government Tourist Office, Toronto, and Holyviews Ltd., Jerusaleum.

Published Quarterly — second class pending.

"The heavens declare the glory of God; And the firmament shows His handiwork. DAY UNTO DAY utters speech, and night unto night reveals knowledge."

— Psalm 19:1,2

Dear Reader,

The phrase, "Day unto day", found in Psalm 19:2, is most meaningful to us all. Our Old Testament devotional commentary writer for this series, Nizar Shaheen, is fluent in the original language of the Old Testament. He tells me that this Hebrew phrase does not just mean "day to day" or "day after day", but rather means "one day flowing into the next without any break". I'm sure this is the way God wants our relationship with Him to be.

Psalm 19:2 is a very special verse to me personally, because God used the words "Day unto day" to speak to me many years ago about the need for daily Christian television and the importance of hearing from God daily through the reading of His Word.

We've entitled this devotional commentary series *Day Unto Day*, after Psalm 19:2. It is designed to guide you through God's Word in two years while giving you fresh devotional thoughts inspired by each day's reading.

This Year One-Spring volume is the second in our eight-volume series. If you did not receive the first volume, the Year One-Winter edition, then you can simply start your two-year journey now and end with volume one in two years time. Please request each volume in writing approximately one month before you'll need it.

My prayer for all who read these volumes is that God's glory will be revealed to you "Day unto Day".

In Christ's love and service,

David Mainse
Host of "100 Huntley Street"

Applying this Guide
to Family Devotions

by Lorne Shepherd
100 Huntley Street's Minister to the Family

Many families have good relationships but do not feel close to one another spiritually. Spiritual oneness is important. In fact, if a husband and wife regularly read the Bible together, pray together, and attend church, their chances of divorce drops from one in two marriages to one in four hundred. Family devotions are important!

However, sometimes it is hard to make daily prayer times a habit. Here are some practical steps that will help you to have a spiritual unity in your family.

1. Read the Bible passage and devotional comments with your family or spouse.

2. Each member of the family should discuss something they received from the devotional.

3. During your day, find a scripture that will bless your mate or family members. Do not preach at one another with scriptures.

4. Pray for each of your family member's needs.

5. Start off slowly. Do not feel you have to pray for half an hour. Time with God should be enjoyable. Expand your devotional time as your relationship with God grows.

6. If you have children, sing a children's chorus and tell a parallel real life story that will help them understand the devotional guide's lessons. Make it fun!

Special Note for Singles — during your day, find someone with whom you can share the principles God has given you during your devotional study.

Introduction

"Day Unto Day" is a new devotional commentary for the nineties! This book is the second of eight volumes which will lead you on a journey through the entire Bible in two years. It's more than a typical daily devotional, and it does not pretend to be an exhaustive commentary. It is designed to lead us deeper and higher into the knowledge of the Almighty God and His Son, the Lord Jesus Christ, through the teaching of the Holy Spirit.

The authors, Jim and Kathy Cantelon with the New Testament and Nizar and Ellen Shaheen, the Old Testament, are uniquely qualified for the task. Both have spent many years in the land of the Bible. Let's meet them now:

Jim Cantelon — Jim was the Pioneer Pastor of the Jerusalem Christian Assembly and remained there for seven years. Prior to going to Jerusalem he served successfully as a Canadian Pastor. His practical application of Scripture was well honed as a popular Canadian open-line radio host. In Jerusalem, he continued on radio covering the Middle East regularly, and became deeply involved in the life of the city as a Rotary Club executive. A most unusual congregation of several hundred members was solidly established. His book, "Theology for Non-Theologians" has had excellent reviews in several leading magazines and is published by MacMillan — the fact that this usually "non-religious" publisher would enthusiastically publish his book is a testimony to what is in store for you in your New Testament readings.

Kathy Cantelon — In Jerusalem she was known as Kathy Kennedy for security reasons. Millions knew her through the nightly television news. Her insightful presentation drew a host of loyal viewers. As the daughter of Rev. and Mrs. E. Howard Kerr, and then a Pastor's wife and mother of three, her down-to-earth insights, joined with those of Jim, her husband, are treasured.

Nizar Shaheen — Here is an Arab native of Israel, perfectly fluent in Arabic and Hebrew, the languages of the Middle East and of the Old Testament. His ancestral family home is in the village of Cana of Galilee, not far from Nazareth where he was born. In his teen years, he became a boxer. He trained by running from Cana to the sea of Galilee, a distance of fifteen miles. Upon arrival at the sea, he would plunge in, swim vigorously, and then return home. Following his miraculous conversion, he applied that same tremendous drive to reading and re-reading the Bible many times a year. Before long, he was ministering extensively in the churches of Israel and the West Bank, as well as preaching and teaching in various countries at seminars and conferences. His study of the ancient culture of peoples of the Middle East have given him most enlightening insights on Old Testament passages. He studied theology in Brussels for four years and received his degree in theology. Today, he hosts an Arabic television program called, "Light for All the Nations" which reaches the immigrant population from Arab countries here in the west and also covers many countries through "Middle East Television". He is known by many who hear him as "a teacher's teacher".

Ellen Shaheen — It was during her undergraduate work at "The American Institute of Holy Land Studies", located on Mount Zion in Jerusalem, that she met Nizar; she met him near the end of eight months of concentration on Biblical Hebrew, Archeology, and historical Geography of the Holy Land. Their marriage in Cana of Galilee was a traditional Middle Eastern wedding. During the ceremony, when Ellen spoke in the language of Cana, Arabic, and said the words of Ruth, "Thy people shall be my people and thy God, my God", the crowd cheered and took her to their heart. Into her participation with Nizar in the writing of the Old Testament devotional commentaries, she brings a liberal arts degree with a Biblical Studies major. She also brings her upbringing in a minister's home, that of her parents, David and Norma-Jean Mainse. This mother of three active children has spent many hours studying with her husband in the preparation and writing of this fresh material.

David and Norma-Jean Mainse — It was in 1962, at 25 and 22 years of age, that they began regular Christian television programming. Now this work continues with the daily "100 Huntley Street" telecast, the children's productions and the many non-English programs. From the TV programs have been birthed Circle Square Ranches for youth across the continent and overseas missions in many countries. God has obviously blessed David and Norma-Jean. They have taken each of the commentaries of Jim and Kathy, Nizar and Ellen and have written a "Prayer for today" which you can use as a short starter for your daily prayer time. In these short prayers, they have used the term "we" rather than "I" because they pray together and are thinking of all who will participate with them in the *Day Unto Day* readings.

May this work be a great blessing to you as you grow stronger in the Lord through reading His Word and prayer — DAY UNTO DAY!

Gologotha — "The place of the skull"
The hill pictured here is believed to be the site of Jesus'
crucifixion because of its skull-like appearance and
its location just outside the walls of Jerusalem.

Introduction to
The Book of Mark

Who was the author of this Gospel? Traditionally, he is seen as the young man whose mother's home was the central meeting place in Jerusalem for the early Christians (Acts 12:12). He was the same "John Mark" who travelled with Barnabas and Saul to Antioch (Acts 12:25), later leaving them at Perga (on the first missionary journey) and returning to Jerusalem (Acts 13:13). Twelve or thirteen years later, he was reconciled to Paul, proving "useful" in an assistant's role (Col.4:10; 2 Tim.4:11; Philemon 24). Most importantly (in terms of the genesis of this book), he was so closely associated with Peter that the apostle referred to him as "Mark, my son" (1 Peter 5:13).

Mark wasn't an apostle as such, but he was intimately knowledgeable about the life and works of Jesus — not just as a young boy looking on, but as a confidant of Peter and a participant in some of the missionary ministries of Paul.

The scholar, F.C.Grant, suggests that Mark's Gospel was written "backwards, from the passion story to the Baptism; for the passion story dominates the narrative almost from the outset" (*The Growth of the Gospels*, Abingdon Press 1933, pp.136-137). There's no question that the servant/martyr, Jesus, dominates this Gospel and lends credence to the common belief of scholars that Mark wrote not to Jews, but to the early Gentile Christians of the Roman empire. These were Christians who were already facing growing persecution and martyrdom for their refusal to worship the emperor/gods of Rome, insisting rather that Jesus of Nazareth was their Lord and King.

This is why many introductions to the Gospel of Mark will draw your attention to chapters 10:43-45 and 8:34-37 as key verses. Mark presents Jesus, not in kingly terms as did Matthew, but as suffering servant (like Isaiah). Jesus serves mankind even to the point of death. The implied question of Mark's Gospel is, "can we do anything less?"

Key Verse: Mark 9:7 *"... This is My beloved Son. Hear Him!"*

Today's reading includes the story of the transfiguration of Jesus as well as a healing of a boy with an evil spirit. It also includes a discussion of who is the greatest among the disciples, and a comment from Jesus on who's with Him and who's against Him. It concludes with a look at the importance of consistent living, especially as it relates to one's example to children. But it's the story of the transfiguration that captures my interest.

Jesus takes Peter, James, and John with Him onto a high mountain (probably Mount Hermon in the north of Israel). There He appears before them with Elijah and Moses, and we read that His clothes become dazzling white, whiter than anyone in the world could bleach them. We are talking here, not about a reflection of light from Jesus, but rather a light emanating from Him. In every sense of the word, this is a transfiguration, a metamorphosis — a total change. And Peter, James, and John see Jesus as no man had ever seen Him before. This is what theologians call a "Christophany", or a manifestation of the Son of God in His true nature as He will be seen on the last day and as He appears now at the right hand of God the Father.

Peter, James, and John could hardly handle it. They were so overwhelmed that the only one who could find words to say was Peter. And, predictably, he says something very human. "Let us put up three shelters: one for You, one for Moses and one for Elijah!" In other words, let's get organized. Let's perpetuate this experience. Let's package it. Let's make it a basis for a religious movement!

While this is happening, Jesus hears a voice saying, "This is My Son whom I love. Listen to Him." Here, God the Father, just as at Jesus' baptism, again affirms Jesus' claims. Then, suddenly, Elijah and Moses disappear. Jesus encourages His disciples to say nothing about this, at least until He rises from the dead. And for once they do keep it to themselves — at least for the time being. But for now, they are captivated with what "rising from the dead" means, especially as it relates to what they have just seen — Moses was dead, Elijah was dead, now they live, and Jesus keeps company with these shining beings! Whatever do you suppose is going on? How can Jesus appear transfigured when He's not dead yet? What will His death mean?

Little did they know that the very death Jesus was about to undergo would result in an open grave which would become the open window for all men and women of faith to enter into the very presence of the eternal Father.

Prayer for today: *Father God, thank You for sending us Your beloved Son. May we truly hear Him as You exhorted us on the mount of transfiguration — hearing Him through our Bible reading and listening in prayer.*

Read Mark 10 April 2

Key Verse: Mark 10:15 *"...Whoever does not receive the kingdom of God as a little child will by no means enter it."*

I think we've all heard it said of some happy senior citizen that he or she is having a "second childhood". Whereas in their early adulthood and middle age they may have been cautious and thoughtful, now they're reckless and irresponsible. For years they were serious and committed to their work; now, all they want to do is have fun. Suddenly they're easily moved emotionally and seemingly over-generous with their money. It's enough to drive their cautious, serious, work-ethic, middle-aged children mad. After all, how do you tell a seventy-five year old to "grow up!"?

What's more, they need their "adult" children's care and wisdom. They're constantly forgetting things — like where their glasses are, or to take their medicine, and they're always going out in the winter-time without their hat and gloves. In a way they've become as dependent on their kids as their kids were once dependent on them.

But that's the wonderful thing about kids. Irresponsible they may be, thoughtless, and playful too — but in all this they are uncritically, unabashedly, thoughtlessly dependent. They not only know how to be cared for, they expect it. It's a natural condition.

The problem with adults is like that of the rich young ruler in this chapter: he was independent. He didn't need anybody. All of us have this independent streak. We want to be our own boss, our own final court of appeal, determining our own boundaries, pursuing our own horizons, unchecked, accountable to, and dependent on, no one. Dependence scares us.

So we strive for money, status, power, whatever it takes to be first. The child is on the bottom rung of the ladder. We want to be on the top rung.

But Jesus, in typical fashion, turns it all around on us. Only the child-like, dependent ones will enter the kingdom of God. And when we do, those who were 'top rung' may find themselves surpassed by the 'bottom-rungers'.

I think it's special that Jesus, in this context, turns to His amazed disciples, and calls them (vs.24), "children". He obviously had a higher view of them than they had of themselves (although I expect they hardly would have chosen the word "children" to describe their grown-up, mature selves). Nevertheless, the point is clear. God calls those who will humble themselves and accept their dependence in a child-like way. Heaven is for children: even the seventy-five year old variety.

Prayer for today: *Dear Lord, please help me to receive your Kingdom in a childlike way and please deliver me from any childishness, that I may grow up into the fullness of Your purpose for my life.*

Read Mark 11 *April 3*

Key Verse: Mark 11:9 *"...Hosanna! Blessed is He who comes in the name of the Lord!"*

Have you ever thought you'd like to be famous? A household name? You know, someone whom people recognize on the street, write articles about and adulate? And, as you fantasize, you undoubtedly see yourself accepting all this adoration rather quietly and modestly. "I don't know what all the fuss is about. I'm just an average person — your everday nice guy." Pretty heady stuff, nonetheless.

But there's something headier still. Being adored is one thing; being *revered* is something else. When adoration turns into worship, you've become a god or goddess — people hang on your every word, emulate you, canonize you. You've joined the elite troop of religious cult leaders and sports heroes. When you speak, people listen, because you speak with authority. The advertisers come to you with lucrative endorsement contracts. The world is your oyster.

So the last thing you want to do is antagonize your admirers. A fan club should be cultivated, not castigated. You want to please them, meet their expectations, fulfil their agenda.

Jesus' admirers had an agenda. It was expressed in the word, "Hosanna!" This shout means, "Save now!", with the emphasis on "now". Many of the Jews in Jesus' day had had enough of Roman occupation. They needed, and looked for, a leader who would rout the Romans and establish the messianic kingdom. Jesus was the answer to their prayers. He had created a stir unlike any other zealot with messianic tendencies. He was a miracle worker, an outspoken teacher, and a charismatic leader of unparalleled magnetism. How ironic that

11

He should enter Jerusalem on a colt! How humble! How sweet would be His ultimate triumph! Or so they thought. But He's got to do it now: the time is ripe. Save now!

It hadn't entered their minds that Jesus had His own agenda. Nor did He need their political support. He was the totally submitted Son of God, who put His Father's will ahead of His own. So, instead of glorying in the adulation and capitulating to the not-so-hidden agenda of the people, Jesus capitalized on the exposure by cleansing the temple area. He didn't cultivate the people, He drove them away, disappointing and angering a lot of fans.

Have you prayed any "Hosannas" lately? "Here's the agenda, Lord. Do it now! Not Your will, but mine be done." And then we wonder why God is strangely silent.

Maybe it's time for you and me to remember Jesus' prayer, "not my will, but *Thine* be done."

Prayer for today: *"Our Father in Heaven, hallowed be Your name. Your kingdom come. **Your will be done on earth as it is in heaven.** Give us this day our daily bread, and forgive us our debts, as we forgive our debtors. And do not lead us into temptation, but deliver us from the evil one. For Yours is the kingdom and the power and the glory forever. Amen."*

Read Mark 12   *April 4*

Key Verse: Mark 12:30 *"...Love the Lord your God with all your heart, with all your soul, with all your mind, and with all your strength..."*

I think we need to establish something right off the top — it's possible to love someone you don't like. Why? Because love is an act of the will, whereas "like" is the product of the emotions. To like someone means to feel good about him, to love someone means to seek his highest good. And you can seek the highest good of the most dislikeable person on earth, if you *choose* to.

In this chapter, Jesus responds to one of the teachers of the law who, impressed with Jesus' debating skills, asks Him which commandment is of most importance. Rather than quoting one of the ten commandments, Jesus refers to Deuteronomy 6:4,5. The greatest commandment, He says, is to love God with all one's heart, soul, mind, and strength. And, in this context, one should love one's neighbour and one's self the same way.

So what do "heart, soul, mind, and strength" refer to? "Heart" obviously refers to the emotions. "Strength" refers to the will. And, "soul and mind", interestingly, are summed up by the scribe in verse 33 (NIV) as "understanding" or intelligence. To summarize, Jesus says we're to love God with all our emotion, intelligence, and will — our feeling, thinking, and doing.

Try to think of your love for God graphically, in terms of three concentric circles (like an archery target). On the outside, the largest and most visible circle is how you feel about God. A little closer to centre is your thinking about Him, and the bull's-eye is what you're doing about that feeling and thinking. Indeed, the core of your love for God is your action. In Jesus' terms, love for God isn't something you say or sing, it's something you do.

Prayer for today: *O Lord, our God, give me grace to truly love You in deed and not in word only. For this purpose I give You my emotions, my intelligence, and my will.*

Read Mark 13 *April 5*

Key Verse: Mark 13:10 *"And the gospel must first be preached to all the nations."*

Prophecy is a hot subject these days. Especially as we've just entered the 1990's, the last decade of this millenium. There are all kinds of self-made prophets out there, ready and more than willing to predict the future. Then there are the Bible prophecy experts, all preaching their interpretations, so various that the sum total is decidedly uncertain at best and confusing at least. What really complicates the picture, though, is that these prophets and their followers tend to take it personally whenever an unbeliever, or proponent of a competing prophetic scheme, questions the validity of their teaching. Some of the most dogmatic opinions extant in Christendom today are those of end-times specialists. For these people, the expression "knowing everything for sure" seems to be axiomatic.

That's why Jesus' words in verse 32 of this chapter are so very vital, "But of that day and hour no one knows, neither the angels in heaven, nor the Son, but only the Father." When God became the man Jesus, He emptied Himself of the independent exercise of His divine attributes — and one of those attributes is omniscience. Jesus, the God/Man, was self-limited. So much so that even He didn't know when the end of the age and the Day of the Lord would be. So if He didn't know, how can we, mere mortals, expect to know? If you want to speculate, do so as an exercise, not as a dogma.

There is, however, one thing Jesus says that tends to be measureable rather than speculative, as we attempt to interpret this chapter. It's the statement in verse 10, "the gospel must first be preached to all the nations". This is something that has never been possible except in the last half of this century. The preaching of the gospel by way of radio and television is reaching more of the world than ever in history. Nevertheless, according to the Lausanne Committee on World Evangelism, there are still thousands of people groups in the world who have never heard the message.

So if you want to expend some energy and embrace a preoccupation that is not counter-productive in this area of prophetic interpretation, try evangelism. The very best thing you can do is speak of Jesus to your neighbour. Jesus, after all, is the Spirit of true prophecy (Rev.19:10b).

Prayer for today: *Lord Jesus, the testimony about yourself is the Spirit of prophesy. Grant to me the great honour of testifying to someone today. Amen!*

Read Mark 14 *April 6*

Key Verse: Mark 14:31 & 50 *"…'If I have to die with You, I will not deny You!' And they all said likewise…then they all forsook Him and fled."*

I can identify with the disciples. They were keen, energetic fellows, with more than their fair share of courage — it takes a brave man to parry the ardent questions and objections of friends, relatives, and a wife concerning a three year stint of irresponsible wandering with a zealot from Galilee. I can just hear Peter's wife asking, "But how do you expect to pay this year's taxes if you don't get back to fishing?" Yes, they were strong on resolve, but were also weak on follow-through. Like me, (and you, perhaps), they were never at a loss for good intentions. Take a look at this chapter.

Here the narrative presents the first events leading to the crucifixion of Jesus. We read of Jesus' dinner with Simon the leper just two days before Passover. It was this meal which was highlighted by the extravagant act of the unnamed woman, pouring expensive perfume on Jesus' head. Then, two days later, Jesus has His last Passover meal with His disciples. As they eat the traditional meal, with its unleavened bread and mandatory four cups of wine, Jesus uses these common elements to symbolize forever His broken body and shed blood. Then comes the noble resolve, and ignoble follow-through, of both Peter and the rest of the crew.

You see it in the key verses (31 and 50). Peter was the spokesman, but they all shared in the disgrace. After pledging undying loyalty, they all "forsook Him and fled". Sounds like something I'd do. Threaten me with the electric chair and I'll back-pedal quickly, especially in the heat of the moment, when the first reflex is self-justification and self-preservation! Like Peter, I might weep bitterly... after. But for now, "I'm out of here!"

Mind you, the speed of the events left the disciples quite breathless (and spineless) — why, even Jesus' enemies couldn't get their act and their stories together (vs.56 & 59). Nevertheless, we have here a tried and true reality in which we all share: the gap between what we say and what we do.

Thank God, even the apostle Paul needed to hear what we need to hear, "My strength is made perfect in weakness." Take it easy on the sinner. There, but for the grace of God, go I.

Prayer for today: *Lord God, please empower us in our daily living so that the gap between what we say and what we do may close. Thank you for Your forgiveness and your overcoming grace which You give to us when we ask.*

Read Mark 15 *April 7*

Key Verse: Mark 15:39 "*... Truly this man was the Son of God.*"

So why are you a Christian? Because you were raised that way? Perhaps it's because of Sunday School, or the witness of a friend. Maybe reading the Bible did it. Whatever. But why a Christian, rather than a Buddhist or Muslim? Why not an atheist? There's only one answer to that: "Jesus". Never in the history of this planet has there ever been such a man. For those who've been confronted by His presence, or who've taken the time to study His ministry and personal claims, there's no neutral ground. You either embrace Him or displace Him. There are no maybe's.

In this chapter we read about the trial, judgment, crucifixion and burial of Jesus. There are several personalities surrounding the central figure — teachers of the law, the Sanhedrin, chief priests, Pilate, the crowd, soldiers, Barabbas, two thieves, Simon the Cyrene, Mary Magdalene, Jesus' own mother Mary, and one Roman centurion. This man wasn't a Christian, yet, but in the maelstrom of Jesus' crucifixion He says something that suggests he may have become a believer later.

Jesus died with the heart-rending cry, "My God, my God, why have you forsaken me?" Unlike the Jews, some of whom would recognize these words as a direct quote from the messianic Psalm 22, and, unlike the theologians who would debate the issue of God forsaking Himself, the centurion is completely gripped by the divinity of this last gasp, and declares, "Surely this man was the Son of God!" The pathos of the cry, and the way in which Jesus died, caused this Gentile soldier to unequivocally accept the claims of the "king of the Jews".

If he were asked later to defend his faith, the centurion may have had no foot to stand on other than his experience of Christ. Years later, he may have had access to some of the early Christian writings. Maybe he even attended one of the churches Paul established in Asia Minor. Who knows?

But one thing we do know. Whether you're a soldier, sailor, tinker or tailor, you can know Jesus and even love Him — mainly because He knew and loved you first. His word undergirds and nourishes faith. But in the final analysis, it's your experience of Christ that sustains you. Call it a lasting relationship.

Prayer for today: *Lord Jesus, reveal Yourself to us anew. May we experience Your reality today. Like the centurion we exclaim, "Truly this was the Son of God". You gave Yourself for us, O Lord, we give ourselves to You for this new day.*

Read Mark 16 *April 8*

Key Verse: Mark 16:6 *"...He is risen! He is not here. See the place where they laid Him."*

One of the most important ingredients in the resurrection of Jesus is the fact of His death. Jesus really died. Just like our ancestors have done. Just like you and I will do. Why is this so important? Here's why.

Please indulge me as I quote from my book, "Theology for Non-Theologians": "...there have been two classic mistakes throughout history whenever Christians have attempted to explain the person of Jesus Christ. One is very practical — 'Jesus simply couldn't have been God.' And the other is very mystical — 'Jesus wasn't really human at all'. Yet the Bible presents Jesus as fully God and fully man. He has two natures united in one person. Most believers have little sympathy for mistake number one, but they do have an affinity with mistake number two. This shouldn't surprise us, for, historically, this dehumanizing of Jesus has always been a major problem for the church." (P.253, Macmillan, N.Y.; Collier Macmillan, London).

Look at the key verse, "He is risen! He is not here. See the place where they laid Him." Notice the words, "here", and "place". These are spatial words. Spirits are both "here" and "there", and no one has ever thought to attempt the burial of a spirit in a "place". Only physical bodies are buried in a place. Usually we mark the place with some kind of memorial. In fact, it is possible to visit the grave sites of some great religious leaders to this day. The point is this: Jesus didn't just vanish, as if He were merely spirit or some kind of super-angel, He died. He had a body — a flesh and blood body, just like you and me. He was all man.

And He was all God. In fact, He was fully man and fully God. At the same time! God/man — the only one of His kind. The grave tells us He was man. The resurrection tells us He was God. And the post-resurrection appearances and final ascension tell us He is "the same, yesterday, today and forever."

So, while He remains the same, we put our trust in Him — and are never the same again.

Prayer for Today: *Dear Lord, because You lived Your life on earth as a man, You truly do understand all our human needs. We give You all our needs today.*

Introduction to

The Book of Leviticus

The laws given in the book of Leviticus were written down by Moses as the Lord commanded Him. They are mainly ceremonial laws which served as a guide for the newly formed Levitical priesthood: hence the name "Leviticus", meaning "that which pertains to the Levites". The Hebrew title is *Wayyiqra*, meaning "And He Called" taken from the first words of the book, but it is commonly called the "Law of the Offerings", and the "Law of the Priests", for it was like a guidebook for the priests. However, much of the content is vital for the life of the common Israelite as well, since in it they are shown how to properly worship, serve, and obey a holy God, for, as the key verse of the whole book states, "You shall be holy, for I the Lord your God am holy" (19:2). In order for this to be fulfilled, the basic rules for holy living are laid down in this book. Every aspect of life was to reflect God's holiness. In fact, the main theme of Leviticus is "holiness", and a corresponding theme is "atonement", for holiness can only be attained by proper atonement through the shed blood of the sacrifice. We can see in this concept, as well as in some of the regulations, that within the book many symbols point to the person and work of Jesus Christ.

In Exodus, Israel was delivered, redeemed, and set apart unto God as a holy nation. In Leviticus, God shows His people how to fulfil their calling of holy service and dedication to Him, much of which were based upon the prescribed holy offerings, rituals, and feasts; then they would be able to have communion with their covenant God. As the covenant people of God, they were exhorted to be distinctly different from the surrounding heathen nations, an emphasis that applies well to believers today as the elect of God. We can learn much from the book of Leviticus, as well as have our faith in Jesus Christ strengthened and come to appreciate more what God has done through Jesus in ushering in the New Covenant of His wonderful grace.

Read Leviticus 1 & 2 *April 9*

Key Verse: Leviticus 1:4 *"Then he shall put his hand on the head of the burnt offering, and it will be accepted on his behalf to make atonement for him."*

When we read about the sacrifices in the book of Leviticus, we must understand two things: the position of God, and the position of the offerer/worshipper. The Most Holy God, full of grace and mercy, summoned Moses, not from the fiery mountain of Sinai but from the tent of meeting upon which the glory of His presence came to rest and dwell in the midst of His covenant people (Ex. 40:34-38). The worshipper was privileged to come with humble reverence into communion with God through the blood of the sacrifice, being made acceptable and reconciled with Him, receiving forgiveness for sins. This theme of atonement ("covering" for sin) is found in the first chapter of Leviticus (1:4) and continues throughout the whole book. The instructions were intended for all the people to hear (1:2), not just the priests, for **all** were welcomed to draw near and commune with God through the means of the sacrificial offering. Rich and poor alike would bring their voluntary gifts out of appreciation for what the Lord had done, be it an expensive bullock, or a simple pigeon. In any case, the sacrifice had cost them something, and was to be willingly and happily given. Jesus stressed the importance of the right motivation and the intent of the heart, only then would any offering be acceptable to God (Matt. 5:23-24; Mark 12:33).

Burnt offerings were to be always offered up to God. They were to be unblemished males, the largest and strongest animal, since perfection was necessary. The offerer was to firmly lay his hand upon the animal's head signifying his identification with it and laying his guilt upon it. The animal's death represented the death the offerer deserved for his own sins. Great care was taken for the blood of the sacrificial animal, since this is all important and necessary for atonement (17:11). It is awful to think of how our Lord Jesus painfully shed His blood, but this was absolutely necessary for our atonement.

No part of the burnt offering was to be eaten, for it was to be totally consumed on the altar, signifying total surrender to God. A great biblical truth is seen in this offering: the people were able to come close to God in worship and have their sins covered — all because of a substitute. Jesus gave Himself as a substitute when He died on the cross. He offered Himself entirely as a sacrifice to God in our place. He was the "sweet aroma to the Lord" (1:9), the perfect substitute, bearing our sin and shame that we might be forgiven and find favour before the most holy God. We, like the Israelites, in response to God's acceptance of that Offering (Jesus), must lead a consecrated life that is pleasing to Him and be cleansed daily.

The **grain or meal offering** (ch. 2) was brought to the tabernacle as a gift, possibly expressing gratitude or reverence to God. This was the only offering that did not involve blood, but it was usually accompanied by an animal offering. A handful of this offering was burnt as a memorial, and all that remained was to be eaten by Aaron and his sons. It also expressed personal dedication to the Lord. In offering it, the worshipper recognized the sovereignty of God, His grace and goodness in giving the fruit of the earth, and his dependence upon Him to sustain life. This offering was to contain no leaven (which pictured sin), but it, like all the other offerings, was to contain salt, representing that which preserved against corruption and added flavour. Salt pictured permanence and was symbolic of the eternal nature of God's covenant (2:13; Num. 18:19). Still today, believers in Jesus who have been purged by His precious blood and are, as the Apostle Paul termed, "living sacrifices" (Rom. 12:1,2), enjoy the covenant relationship with God and are, as Jesus said, "the salt of earth" (Matt. 5:13).

Prayer for today: *Lord God, we present our bodies as living sacrifices according to the grace you've given unto us. Thank you very, very much that Your hand of judgement for sin was laid firmly on Him at the altar of the cross so that we who believe are set free from the penalty of sin.*

Read Leviticus 3 & 4   *April 10*

Key Verse: Leviticus 4:21 *"Then he shall carry the bull outside the camp, and burn it.... It is a sin offering for the assembly."*

The **peace offering** was a beautiful voluntary expression of the Israelites' gratitude toward God. It was offered to publically recognize God's goodness for His blessings and to express love, thanks, and praise to Him. The Hebrew word for the offering is "shalom", meaning "peace" or "wholeness". The result of the offering was to be peace between God and man, and wholeness or peace within one's soul. This offering has been translated as the "fellowship offering" (N.I.V), since it was the only one from which the worshipper might eat a portion along with the officiating priest. On occasion it could be shared with friends in a holy gathering, thus allowing fellowship with God and other believers. The greatest sacrifice, Jesus Christ, has now become the believer's peace (Ephesians 2:13,14), for it is only through Him that we receive mercy, forgiveness, true inner peace, and fellowship with God.

Certain fatty parts of this sacrifice were not to be eaten by anyone, but were to be burned on the altar (3:11,16), becoming a sweet aroma unto God. This is the Lord's portion alone, for "all the fat is the Lord's" (3:16), as is the all important blood, therefore no one was to eat from them (3:17). This warning is stressed seventeen times in the Book of Leviticus. God gave this law, and many others, not only for symbolic significance, but for ensuring the health of His people and teaching obedience.

The **sin offering** was a mandatory sacrifice for the purpose of atonement for specific sins done unintentionally, or in ignorance. Since all people, as sons of Adam, have a sinful nature, the sin offering was required for the resulting guilt and defilement. It required a confession of sin and was to result in forgiveness and cleansing. However, it was not merely the external act of sacrificing that brought atonement. Rather, as the New Testament teaches, and even some Jewish commentators express, the sin offering was only effectual to make atonement for those who were truly repentant and had faith that God was able to bring about their atonement.

Jesus seemed to allude to mankind's unintentional sinning in His prayer while on the cross, "Father, forgive them, for they do not know what they do" (Luke 23:34). We, as believers today, need to learn more of God and His Word and to ask the Holy Spirit to quicken our spirits and write His laws upon our hearts and minds (Heb. 10:16) that we may not fall into sin. Most importantly, we need to always plead the blood of Jesus to cover our sin. As the writer of the epistle to the Hebrews stressed, sin could not be taken away by the blood of bulls and goats (Hebrews 10:4), but "with His own blood He [Jesus] entered the Most Holy Place once for all, having obtained eternal redemption" (Hebrews 9:12). Jesus Christ is the true sin offering whose blood cleanses from **all** sin for which the old covenant's sacrificial system was inadequate (e.g. Numbers 15:30).

When the high priest sinned, and thus brought guilt upon all the Israelite people whom he represented (4:3), or when the whole congregation of Israel was guilty of sinning unintentionally (4:13), the sin offering was to be a young, unblemished bull, the most costly of any sacrifice. Only on such an occasion and on the day of Atonement the blood of the sacrifice was sprinkled seven times (the number of perfection) before the veil of the sanctuary. This sin offering was not to be eaten by any priest, as it was in other cases, but after burning the fat, and kidneys of the bull, all the rest was to be taken outside the camp and burned (4:12,21). The writer of the epistle to the Hebrews clearly shows a parallel here: "Jesus also, that He might sanctify the people with His own blood, suffered outside the gate" (Heb. 13:12). Indeed, Jesus was crucified on Golgatha, outside the city walls of Jerusalem, and it is to Him we must go; to a place despised in the world's eyes, but made holy by His presence and His wonderful work of atonement.

Prayer for today: *Almighty God, we worship You and we partake by faith of the peace offering made by Your Son and our Saviour. May our lives show forth the peace that You have provided by the blood of the cross. (Col.1:20)*

Read Leviticus 5 & 6 *April 11*

Key Verse: Leviticus 5:5 *"And it shall be, when he is guilty in any of these matters, that he shall confess that he has sinned in that thing".*

We are told in chapter five of specific instances when **the sin offering** was required. In the old covenant period, a faithful and true witness was very important, since their justice depended upon it and they had no signed contracts as we do today; it was considered a sin if the witness did not testify to the truth (5:1). Another guilty verdict was pronounced upon the one who became ceremonially unclean; even if it happened unknowingly, a sin offering was still required (5:2-3). Lack of separation from the "unclean" things of the world can likewise defile a believer today. It is a great spiritual challenge and a mark of "pure and undefiled religion before God..."to keep oneself unspotted from the world" (James 1:27). When we find we have become tainted with wordly things, we also must ask forgiveness and seek atonement.

A third instance we read here that required a sin offering was when a rash and thoughtless oath was sworn. What is demanded here is self-control. The Apostle James gave a warning about the powerful instrument of the tongue (James 3:5-6) and the Book of Proverbs is full of wise sayings about it (Proverbs 10:19; 13:3; 15:4; 21:23). It is clearly taught in the Bible that we must watch our words and let all we say be glorifying to the Lord.

Provision was made for **all people** to approach God with their sin offering. Nobody was excluded; the very poor Israelites who could not afford two birds were still able to bring fine flour, and with their hearts right before God, atonement would be made for their sin. Today we see that no one is excluded from the salvation available through the sacrifice of Jesus.

We learn that, before the sin offering was effectual, it had to be accompanied by the offerer's **confession** to God of the particular sin; if this was not done, there could be no atonement. This principle of confession for atonement is consistent with the New Covenant teaching as well: "If we confess our sins, He is faithful and just to forgive us" (1 John 1:9). No oil or incense was to be used with the sin offering, for these ingredients represented joy and the one asking forgiveness should be sorrowful for the sin. However, the sorrow disappears when God's forgiveness is received.

The sin offering and the trespass or guilt offering are very similar. The difference is that **the trespass offering** was brought when restitution was required (5:16; 6:4,5), like repaying a neighbour for some harm done (6:1-7). Trespassing against the Lord in regard to the holy things (5:14-19) probably means that the offender failed to give to God His rightful tithes, offerings, first fruits, or ransom money (Ex. 30:11-16). The restitution was to pay back what was originally owed, along with an additional 20 percent, and the offering of an unblemished ram. Such transgressions required that atonement be made, then the Lord promised to forgive (5:18). No doubt there are many who claim to follow Christ today, yet fail to give God His share. Forgiveness must be sought by such persons.

Finally, directions are given concerning the priest's own use of the burnt, grain, and sin offerings. Respecting God's commands in all areas of service to Him is necessary, for the true meaning of the sacrifice could be lost if the various rituals were not properly observed. Great care was to be taken of the priest's clothing, disposing of the ashes and, very importantly, the fire on the altar was to burn continually. The priest, as the people's representative to God, was to ensure that there were always uninterrupted appeals going up to the Lord on behalf of both the priesthood and the whole assembly of Israel. The priests and the high priest were not exempt from offering sacrifices to the Lord on their own behalf. They, probably more than any of the common people because of their responsibility, were to confess their sins, keep pure, give offerings, and remain in constant fellowship with God. However, because our great High Priest, Jesus Christ, was perfect and sinless, atonement through Him is much more effective (Hebrews 7:25-26).

Prayer for today: *Lord God, thank You that a continual sacrifice, Your Lamb, is there at the altar in heaven and that His intercession continually is before You. (Hebrew 7:25)*

Read Leviticus 7 *April 12*

Key Verse: Leviticus 7:6 *"Every male among the priests may eat it. It shall be eaten in a holy place. It is most holy."*

In the Old Covenant period, only the males from the priestly families were consecrated to the Lord and His service, and only they were permitted to enter the holy places and eat from the holy offerings. All the offerings consecrated to the Lord, especially those for the expiation of sin, were considered most holy. God does not take sin lightly, nor should we. It is a serious matter and must be dealt with. That is why God established the sacrificial system until His Son Jesus became the final, perfect, and ultimate Sacrifice, through whom we receive forgiveness of sins. All believers in the New Covenant, whether male or female, who are totally consecrated to the Lord make up the body of His holy priesthood, and as such may partake of the very holy things of the Lord. All true followers of Jesus may enter directly into the holy presence of the Lord and share in His Holy Communion, the Lord's Supper; all may partake of the spiritual food received from the Holy Bible; all may receive spiritual gifts and fruits bestowed by the Holy Spirit. The Lord God is certainly a giver of great gifts, the greatest of which was His Son.

This chapter relates further information about the trespass and peace offering. The wave and heave offerings (7:30,32) were portions of that offering which were voluntarily given for those who served God. The act of waving the breast portion of the sacrifice up before God signified consecration to Him and, in the heave offering, the right thigh was first lifted up toward God and then given into the priest's hands for his personal use. In these and other ways, God saw to it that His priests shared in His offerings. This was one way they received pay for the great service they performed continually. Although only the priests could partake of the holy offerings in the holy place, they could still provide for their wives and families because the first fruits and tithes, as well as the breasts and right thighs of the peace offerings could be taken to their homes. These offerings enabled the priests not to worry about having to work elsewhere and earn a living so they could devote all their time to the service of God (cf.1 Corinthians 9:13,14). As it was then, and still is today, it is the responsibility of the Lord's people to support those who serve God in full-time ministry (1 Tim. 5:16,17).

More details concerning the nature of the peace offering is given from verses 11 to 35. Three types are described, all having to do with communion with God. (1) A thanksgiving offering, (2) a vow offering, and (3) a freewill or voluntary offering which sprang from joy in the covenant relationship with God. It was strictly required that no meat of the offering became defiled by leaving it longer than the specified time. If this was disobeyed and the offering was eaten, it would be unacceptable to God and the offender would be guilty (7:18). Guilt also came upon the person who, being ceremonially unclean, ate from the holy offering. This disobedience resulted in exile or possibly death, being "cut off from his people". It was a serious matter, for those things holy to the Lord are sacred and must be respected. It is similar with the Lord's Supper today (1 Corinthians 11:27-29). We as the Lord's priests are to be holy, as He is holy (Leviticus 19:2; 1 Peter 1:15,16). To be holy there must be obedience to the Lord. It is once again stressed in chapter seven that the Israelites were to eat no fat or blood, and again there is a serious penalty: being "cut off". These rules, like many others given, including the burning of the offered meat on the third day (7:17), were good for the health of the people, for they were living in a hot desert region.

A basic principle of atonement was set forth: the offering was to be brought personally to the tabernacle by the person offering it, never by proxy (7:30). Asking God for forgiveness, dedicating oneself to Him, giving thanks to Him and having communion with Him was to be done by the individual worshipper as a tangible response to God's blessings. Mere words expressing thanks or love were not enough; it had to be done "in deed and in truth" (1 John 3:18). Sacrificial material and financial gifts to the work of the Lord were the proper Isrealite response to their love of God. This response should be ours today.

Prayer for today: *O Lord, help us to offer sacrificial gifts to You. We trust You for forgiveness and now we offer a tangible expression of our thankfulness.*

Read Leviticus 8 & 9   *April 13*

Key Verse: Leviticus 9:6 *"... This is the thing which the Lord commanded you to do, and the glory of the Lord will appear to you."*

Now that God had instructed Moses about all the various offerings, it was time for them to be put into effect. Firstly, the offerings were made ready (8:1,2), then the priests, as God's representatives, had to be purified with water and properly attired (8:6-9), sanctified by anointing (8:10-12; for review see commentaries on Ex.28,29), forgiven of their sin through offering sacrifices of atonement (8:14-17), and consecrated by the offering of the ram. The blood of the ram was applied to the priest's right ear, right thumb, and right large toe, signifying they should hear God's word, do God's work, and walk in God's ways. Their seven-day stay worshipping the Lord in the tabernacle was a further sign of complete consecration. This elaborate ceremony was performed in front of the whole assembly of Israel, just as the Lord had commanded. It was necessary for these rites to be seen in public so that the people might have greater reverence for the Lord and the priests who were to intercede on their behalf.

It was important and necessary that Moses, ordained by God, preside over the inauguration ceremonies. Although he was not, in the strictest sense of the word, a priest, he was at that time the only mediator between God and man, and thus was appointed by God to be the first to do these priestly functions and thereby show Aaron and his sons the proper procedures. Moses was obedient to all the Lord's commands and was really acting on behalf of God in consecrating the newly formed priesthood.

Once Aaron and his sons had been obedient to the Lord (8:36) and the important seven days of consecration had been completed, Moses called them out (9:1) and here started the full-fledged sacred work of the sacrificial rites. Before Aaron and his sons could minister on behalf of the people, they themselves needed to bring offerings (9:2). For a priest to properly minister to others he must first take care of his own spiritual well-being. Once he had done this, he could see to the people's offerings. The priest's role was very important in the Israelite community: to make atonement through the blood sacrifice and teach the people in the ways of God, as well as enforcing the Law of God. They were to be a holy people, set apart to God's service.

The order of the sacrifices brought by the people is significant and demonstrates the basic principles of worship to God. Firstly, the sin offering was brought for the forgiveness of sins. Secondly, the burnt offering signified commitment and dedication to God. Thirdly, the grain offering represented thankfulness and joy, since those who have repented of sin and are consecrated to God have great reason to be joyful. Finally, with all this accomplished the peace offering signified communion or fellowship with God. All this became available because of the blood of the sacrifice. Once sin has been removed and the individual's life is devoted to God, communion with Him is made possible.

Moses' had spoken with great faith when he declared that after the Lord's commands were obeyed His glory would appear (9:6).

Indeed, when everything had been done in obedience to God, and after Moses and Aaron had blessed the people, God's glory was manifested by holy fire descending and consuming the offerings, showing His presence, acceptance and pleasure. The fire of God will not fall unless all is done in obedience to Him. This has implications in the life of believers today, as well as for the church.

Prayer for today: *Lord Jesus, in Your once-and-for-all sacrifice You provided all our needs. On this basis we ask afresh for forgiveness, commitment to You, and fellowship with You.*

Read Leviticus 10 *April 14*

Key Verse: Leviticus 10:3 *"...By those who come near Me I must be regarded as holy; and before all the people I must be glorified..."*

Immediately following the people's awestruck response, as they prostrated themselves and worshipped God in fear and reverence because of the divine manifestation of God's glory by the miraculous fall of fire (10:2), we read of the tragic incident with Aaron's sons, Nadab and Abihu. The same fire from God which signified His acceptance and pleasure in the sacrificial offerings became a weapon of His wrath and justice against something which very much displeased Him.

What had Nadab and Abihu done to provoke God to such a drastic measure? (1) The most obvious reason we find stated in the Bible is that they offered profane or strange fire before the Lord which was in disobedience to Him (10:1). It was not the holy fire taken from the bronze altar of burnt offering which the Lord Himself had kindled. (2) Then they each brought their own censers, not the one which had been sanctified and especially made for use in the tabernacle. Only things consecrated for holy service were allowed inside the holy place. (3) Also, both men offered the incense together, whereas only one was to do this, and that was the high priest. By doing this, they deliberately and disobediently took upon themselves the duty reserved for the high priest. They may have done this because of pride or arrogance in their new privileged position. They should have been all the more humble before God since, on one special occasion, they had been permitted to ascend Mt. Sinai and, from a distance, see God's glory (Ex. 24:1).

(4) Another possible reason contributing to their death is that they may have been intoxicated (drunk), for immediately after this incident, the Lord gave a strong warning against any priest drinking

alcohol when it is his time to go into the tabernacle, "lest you die" (10:9). The Lord's instructions are to be carried out properly and thoughtfully which drunkenness would prevent, along with this is the reason: "that you may distinguish between holy and unholy, and between unclean and clean" (10:10). They were also not to drink so that they may fulfil their important role of teaching their children (both natural and spiritual children) all the ways of the Lord, as well as being a good example and living above reproach. Does this passage not have significance for believers today, those who are the Lord's "royal priesthood" (1 Peter 2:9), who are continually in His presence?

This event serves as a warning to all who are dedicated to God's service. The things of the Lord and His holiness are not to be taken lightly. Certainly Aaron and his remaining two sons, Eleazar and Ithamar, were greatly affected by this tragedy. They could speak no words of complaint, and Aaron was submissive because the Lord's judgments are just — "So Aaron held his peace"; God is holy and must be regarded as such when approached (see key verse, 10:3). It could have been out of fear that Aaron and his sons did not eat from the sin offering, thus angering Moses (10:16). It is possible that they were afraid to eat the holy food, in case they, too, were unworthy or unclean, and being sorrowful at the loss of their brothers, they must have had no appetite and may have felt they were not in the right attitude to partake of the holy offering (10:19). Rather than letting it remain and see corruption, they burnt it totally. With Aaron's explanation, Moses' anger was appeased. Though Aaron and his two sons were disobedient, this time God was merciful, compassionate, and understanding, for it appears they were not punished.

Prayer for today: *Grant us, O Lord, Your favour because of our Lord Jesus. "Dressed in His righteousness alone, faultless to stand before the throne." We spend time in Your holy presence.*

Read Leviticus 11 & 12 *April 15*

Key Verse: Leviticus 11:45 *"For I am the Lord who brings you up out of the land of Egypt, to be your God. You shall therefore be holy, for I am holy."*

After the terrible blight upon the new priesthood (10:1), and after Moses' rebuke (10:17,18), the Lord reassured and honoured Aaron in his high priestly position by speaking directly to him along with Moses. Aaron was to have great respect from all the people because of the position God had given him. It was necessary for Aaron to hear these regulations since he was given the responsibility of teaching the people. God gave instructions regarding foods that were clean and unclean. He was concerned for the spiritual and physical well-being of His people. We must understand that the Israelites had lived under the poor conditions of slavery in Egypt. They had much to learn, and their loving God of the covenant had their best interests in mind and was certainly the one to give the wisest laws. These distinctions between clean and unclean foods had been known to a certain degree in the time of Noah (Genesis 7:2). This knowledge had probably been passed down verbally throughout the generations. No doubt God instructed Adam about these regulations, but over the centuries and during the many years in Egypt, they may have become careless. However, now with their new covenant relationship with God and their new honoured position as God's holy nation, they needed more specific laws to clearly show them to be a distinct nation, a people set apart for God as a holy and pure people.

The basic guidelines God gave His people were: concerning animals, only those that chewed the cud and had a split hoof (11:3) were permitted to be eaten; from the water, only creatures with fins and scales were to be eaten (11:9). Birds and insects were also covered; neither birds of prey nor most insects were to be consumed (11:13-23). After making these demands, God gave the reason they were to obey; simply because He was their God and deliverer who brought them out of bondage; He was holy and, therefore, they too were to be holy (11:44,45).

These sound health and sanitary principles were especially needed at that time of Israel's history. They were travelling in a desert area, constantly exposed to the elements and to wildlife of all sorts. In such an area, sickness could be easily transmitted. Following the Lord's instructions would not only lead to better physical health but, even more importantly, to better spiritual health. If observed carefully, these laws would serve as a constant reminder to the Israelites that they were to be a separated and holy nation. In obeying God and keeping themselves pure they were in a better position to have communion with Him. When we obey and honour the Lord, and are nourished with the spiritual food found in God's Holy Bible, we too will also can have better fellowship with God and grow in Him.

In Chapter 12, we learn that the Israelite women were ceremonially unclean for a period of time after childbirth, meaning they could not participate in the worship activities at the tabernacle. A possible reason for this may be related to mankind's sinful nature which is imparted to a child at conception. However, in the Old

Covenant, having children was considered a joy and a blessing from God (Psalm 127:3-5), and in obedience to His command to "be fruitful and multiply" (Genesis 1:28; 9:7). It is a serious consideration to bring into the world children who will, by nature, inherit the depravity of sin, but God gave a hope for man's restoration to Him which was symbolized in the offerings the new mother would bring after her time of uncleanness was over. Curiously, this time period was twice as long for a girl baby as it was for a boy. It may be that the time was shortened because of the boy's rite of circumcision on the eighth day, symbolizing the covenant relationship with God (12:3; Genesis 17:12).

Today we do not need to worry about following these specific ceremonial laws, since they do not apply to us (see 1 Timothy 4:3-5). The Apostle Paul, speaking of the ceremonial law, wrote that Jesus "has taken it out of the way, having nailed it to the cross" (Colossians 2:14, see also verses 16,17). We do, however, need to concern ourselves with being obedient to God and keeping ourselves pure, holy, and undefiled in a world full of uncleanness (1 Peter 1:14, 15). It is only by the power of Jesus Christ and His Holy Spirit within us that we can live a holy life.

Prayer for today: *Almighty God, we ask for Your work of holiness in our lives. Grant us the grace to obey You, to keep ourselves pure, holy and undefiled. We pray this in Jesus' all powerful Name, Amen!*

Read Leviticus 13 *April 16*

Key Verse: Leviticus 13:46 *"He shall be unclean. All the days he has the sore he shall be unclean. ... he shall dwell alone; his habitation shall be outside the camp."*

Once again, the Lord spoke with Moses and Aaron concerning important health matters. These regulations in chapter 13 were designed to protect the people and control the spread of one of the most terrible and dreaded diseases, leprosy. It is not certain whether the Israelites at that time knew if it was contagious or not (however God did), for it seems that the disease is referred to as making one ceremonially unclean. Lepers were separated from the camp so that others might not come in contact with them, thus becoming ceremonially unclean themselves and therefore unable to participate in community life or go to the tabernacle for worship.

It appears that various other diseases, as well as the leprosy we know of today, are discussed here, but all are put under the general name "leprosy", even mildew in garments or leather (13:47). Great care was taken to distinguish if the affliction was only the appearance of leprosy, or actually entailed the individual's total separation, or, in the case of material, being burned (13:52). Upon close examination by a priest, the one in question was either 1) isolated for a period of seven days (13:26, 50; signifying a complete period of time for observation); 2) separated totally if the diagnosis was positive (13:46), or 3) if negative, returned to normal life and activities, including tabernacle worship.

The Israelites had such a strong belief in the sovereignty of God that someone having leprosy or another infirmity was considered under the judgment of God because of sin. In the Bible, there are several instances of this happening as a direct result of sin (with Miriam, Nu.12:10; Gehazi, 2 Kings 5:25-27; and Uzziah, 2 Chronicles 26:18-21). In fact, this idea was evident even in the New Testament. We see Jesus being questioned concerning the blind man, "who sinned, this man or his parents, that he was born blind?" Jesus answered, "neither...but that the works of God should be revealed in him" (John 9:2,3). Probably this was a totally new way for the Jews to view an affliction. Jesus certainly taught new things and brought much change.

If one was found to have a real case of leprosy, drastic measures were immediately taken to separate him from society. Firstly, his clothes were to be torn, his hair unkept, and a covering was to be put over his upper lip; all were signs of mourning (cf. Ezekiel 24:17,22). It was as if he had died, and he was to call out, "unclean, unclean", if anyone came in his path. The disease may have been considered incurable, since there is nothing said about the means of healing it, but there was provision for a purification ritual when one was found to be clean (chapter 14). This would imply that being cleansed was thought to be an act of divine intervention. Jesus, the greatest example of divine intervention, is said to have cleansed lepers, not cure them.

Leprosy could be considered a type or picture of sin in many ways: (1) it starts from the inside and only later appears outwardly; (2) it is a filthy, loathsome disease; (3) it is difficult to cure; (4) it begins small and seemingly insignificant, but eventually leads to death. Leprosy of the soul should be more dreaded than the actual disease, for it ultimately leads to eternal death and suffering. It defiles the heart and conscience which only Jesus Christ can cleanse by the power of His grace. The Israelite priest could only convict the leper, but Christ, whose holy priesthood greatly transcends his, can cleanse and cure the leper, be it a physical, or spiritual healing. We read of a leper who approached Jesus to worship Him. He said, "Lord, if You are willing, You can make me clean." Then Jesus did what no one else would do, He reached out and touched the man, saying, "I am willing; be cleansed" (Matthew 8:2,3). In the same manner, Jesus is willing today to touch and cleanse from sin anyone who might come to Him. If God's mercy had not been extended through Jesus Christ, then we all would be unclean and unworthy of communion with Him. The Law only shows us our disease, but the Gospel of Jesus Christ shows us our hope and help in Him.

Prayer for today: *Lord Jesus, You once cleansed ten lepers and told them to show themselves to the priest, and only one returned to give You thanks after healing was evident. Thank You Jesus for Your deliverance from the leprosy of sin in our lives. Thank You! Thank You! (Luke 17:12-19)*

Read Leviticus 14   *April 17*

Key Verse: Leviticus 14:20b *"So the priest shall make atonement for him, and he shall be clean."*

Here we see that it was possible for of a leper to be restored to health, cleanness, and communal life, as provision was made for his cleansing. The healing of such awful diseases was attributed to the grace and mercy of God. The ceremony of purification was elaborate and spiritually significant: everything was geared to bringing the former leper back into a place of fellowship with God and the community. Jesus, Himself, after miraculously cleansing the leper instructed him to show himself to the priest and "offer the gift that Moses commanded, as a testimony to them" (Matthew 8:4). He gave another reason for the purification ritual, that it might be a testimony for the glory of God.

On the day the priest found the leper to be clean, two birds were brought to the priest; one was killed, possibly symbolizing the death of the leprosy, the other was set free, symbolizing the person's new freedom. He could now return to his rightful place among his people and to the tabernacle of worship. The sprinkling seven times with the blood mixed with water represented complete purification. Cedar wood, a piece of scarlet cloth and hyssop (probably the herb marjoram) were employed in the purification ritual for both the person and the house which was found rotting with some form of mildew (14:4, 49). The psalmist David probably had this purification ritual in mind when he pleaded to the Lord, "purge me with hyssop, and I shall be clean", indicating his desire to be cleansed from sin.

On the eighth day after the priest pronounced him clean, three lambs were to be sacrificed for the trespass, sin, and burnt offerings. Along with each was offered a grain offering (14:10), which served to express gratitude to God and dependence upon Him to sustain life. The trespass offering was always for restitution. In this case, it may have been offered as a restitution for all the sacrifices and tithes that the leper had been unable to make during his uncleanness. As a former outcast, it is doubtful he could bring all these offerings himself, but doubtless his friends and family were pleased to help provide these offerings and welcome him back into their family and community. In the same way, when a sinner repents, he should be happily welcomed into the family of God.

For those who were poorer, the lambs for the sin and the burnt offering could be substituted with clean birds, but the trespass offering always had to be a male lamb. The solemn ritual was the same since both rich and poor are alike in the presence of God. In our own circles of fellowship, rich and poor should be received in the same way.

Following the sacrifices, the healed leper being cleansed was anointed with blood and oil in much the same manner as the anointing of the priests for service, and the meaning was the same: he should hear God's word, do God's work and walk in God's ways. Today, cleansing from defilement and restoration to communion with God is attained only by asking and receiving forgiveness through Jesus Christ. We who have been cleansed by the blood of Jesus and brought into communion with God must, like the restored leper, not live in seclusion from the brethren. Rather, we must have fellowship with the body of believers, for with this comes the strengthening of faith and spiritual maturity.

Prayer for today: *O Lord, help us today to examine ourselves and properly understand the final and totally complete sacrifice of Jesus for our cleansing and entering into the fellowship of your Church.*

Read Leviticus 15 *April 18*

Key Verse: Leviticus 15:31 *"Thus you shall separate the children of Israel from their uncleanness, lest they die in their uncleanness when they defile My tabernacle that is among them."*

This is an important and practical section of the Israelite code dealing with personal hygiene. More importantly, however, the main purpose of these rulings was that their separation from the surrounding heathen nations and ceremonial holiness would be upheld. It was given by God to teach them, giving specific details as to how a person could become ceremonially unclean because of certain discharges. These requirements promote a constant recognition of God and His holiness in all areas of life. If one was unclean, this meant he or she could not enter the tabernacle, nor participate in the activities there. These ceremonial laws are no longer in effect today, as we are in the New Covenant era, but we can learn certain principles as we remember that all Scripture is God-breathed (2 Timothy 3:16).

If there was an unnatural discharge of some sort from a man or woman (from infections, hemorrhaging, or a woman's prolonged menstruation) then they, and everything they came into direct contact with, would be unclean until seven days after it had stopped. Then they were to wash in running water and bring the prescribed offerings (15:13,14). For the natural discharges, no offerings were necessary; they were only to wash. In the case of a man, he would remain unclean until the next sunset; in the case of a woman, her uncleanness would last for seven days.

In the Gospel of Matthew, we read of a woman who had suffered from an unnatural flow of blood for twelve years. She was therefore unclean and could not participate in religious activites, nor could she touch anyone without making them ceremonially unclean as well. Greatly desiring to be restored to communion with God, she rightly perceived this was available through Jesus, so she took the risk of touching the hem of His garment. Our compassionate Lord not only made her well, but cleansed her (Matt. 9:20-22).

Following the natural act of marriage, the couple were to bathe and then remain unclean until the next sunset. This was to be taken into consideration, since much of community life was involved with worship at the tabernacle. It by no means implies that the marriage act is impure; on the contrary, the Bible teaches that the marriage bed is undefiled (Hebrews 13:4). It does necessitate occasional restraint and self-control in this area (Exodus 19:15), considering the things of God first and foremost. In this way, one's life is kept in balance and in right perspective.

The key verse (verse 31) is addressed directly to the priest. It put great responsibility upon them to teach these regulations, lest anyone in an unclean state enter the tabernacle and thereby defile it, bringing death through God's justice and wrath. Just as uncleanness separated the Israelites from God, so does sin separate us from Him. Sin is the worst type of uncleanness, for unless atonement is made and forgiveness received, it leads to eternal death. It is a terrible thing to die in sin, but we have been adequately warned by God through His Word concerning those things which bring defilement, and He has graciously provided, through Jesus Christ, a way of cleansing. For "who may stand in His holy place? He who has clean hands and a pure heart" (Psalm 24:3,4). Jesus Himself said, "Blessed are the pure in heart, for they shall see God" (Matthew 5:8).

Prayer for today: *Lord God, grant us the gift of Your grace so that we may be separated unto You, not touching the uncleanness of sin. Keep us pure, O Lord.*

Read Leviticus 16   *April 19*

Key Verse: Leviticus 16:21 *"Aaron shall lay both his hands on the head of the live goat, confess over it…all their sins, putting them on the head of the goat."*

We read here of the **Day of Atonement** which could be considered the climax of the Old Covenant's sacrificial system, for it was the most important and solemn ceremonial day of the whole year. In Hebrew it is known as "Yom Kippur" and in the Jewish calendar it comes on the tenth day of the seventh month, the month called Tishri (October).

From verses 29 and 31 we learn that work was prohibited no matter which day of the week Yom Kippur fell. We also learn that their having a proper attitude was important, for they were told, "you shall afflict your souls", meaning they were to be in anguish over their sin, as well as to humble or deny themselves, probably expressed through fasting (cf. Isaiah 58:3,5). This was the only day of fasting that Moses required.

God gave Moses precise instructions to be carefully followed on this special day. It was to be the only day the high priest alone could enter into the Most Holy Place and a strict warning was given for Aaron to obey, "lest he die" (16:2). There was only one way of entrance through the inner veil into the Most Holy Place where the presence of God was manifest above the gold mercy seat, and that was through the blood of the sacrifice. We learn from the Day of Atonement that man has no access to God except through the shed blood of a sacrifice (Hebrews 9:22). Unless our sins are remitted through the atoning work of Jesus Christ, there is no approach to God.

Firstly, Aaron was to remove his ornate high priestly attire, wash his body, and dress in a simple, pure white linen garment. Before he was able to intercede for the people, he was to sacrifice a bull for his own sins and the sins of his household (in contrast to Christ, Hebrews 7:26,27). He was to be totally clean, made holy and acceptable, before he could approach the presence of God (16:6,11). With the blood of the sacrificed bull and the incense to cloud over the mercy seat, Aaron entered the Most Holy Place. The burning incense represented the prayers of the people (and surely praying is what the people were doing who were waiting in anticipation outside). The cloud which resulted was to perhaps veil the glorious manifestation of the Lord from the priest's sight, so that he might not die (16:12,13; Exodus 33:20).

Afterward, one of the two goats was sacrificed for the people and Aaron entered a second time into the Most Holy Place with its blood to make atonement for the people and to cleanse the Holy Place, the tabernacle, and finally the bronze altar because of the people's sins. He sprinkled the blood seven times to symbolize complete purification.

After the first goat had been offered, all the sins of Israel were confessed over the live goat's head as Aaron, their representative, firmly pressed his hands upon it (16:21). The one who takes the blame for the wrong of others is called the scapegoat. In the Hebrew text, this word is "azazel" which most likely is derived from the root meaning "go", or "go away", implying "complete removal". Sending the scapegoat away into the wilderness symbolized that it was bearing away all the sins of the people. It served to make evident the great and gracious work of God's atonement.

These two goats are a foreshadowing of Christ's sacrificial death and of His bearing away sin. Here the scapegoat bore away the sins for **the nation** of Israel, but the most perfect, complete, and final sacrifice, Jesus Christ, who was sent because of God's great love for the whole world, is "the Lamb of God who takes away the sin of **the whole world**" (John 1:29). In fact, the entire Day of Atonement pointed to the day of the Messiah's eternal removal of sin (Zechariah 3:8,9; Hebrews 10:14). For believers, the Day of Atonement was the day our Lord Jesus suffered on the cross outside of the city gate to make a holy, sanctified people through His own blood (Hebrews 13:12). This He did once and for all, unlike the imperfect sacrificial system of the Old Covenant when atonement was made year after year (Hebrews 9:7,12).

Christ secured access into the very presence of God, not only for Himself (Hebrews 9:11,12,24), but for all His followers as well

(Hebrews 10:19-22). In the first three gospels we read that all this was symbolized by the inner veil of the temple that was torn in two from top to bottom (Matthew 27:51; Mark 15:38; Luke 23:45). Christ's death and the torn veil signify that from that time onward mankind was living under the new covenant of grace.

Prayer for today: Lord Jesus, because You are The Eternal High Priest, we can come boldly to the Throne of Grace. May we never neglect the privilege of entering the Holy of Holies where we have an audience with You, O God.

Read Leviticus 17 & 18   *April 20*

Key Verse: Leviticus 18:5 *"You shall therefore keep My statutes and My judgments, which if a man does, he shall live by them: I am the Lord."*

Two strict laws were given by God in chapter 17. Firstly, all sacrifices were to be slaughtered at the door of the tabernacle. The result of this restriction would be: (1) to unify the nation around one place of worship; (2) to remind the people that proper worship of God was done through following His commands; and (3) to prevent any independent worship or sacrificing which could lead to bad influences of pagan practices, such as sacrificing to devils or pagan gods (17:7). Israel had adopted much idolatry in Egypt and this had to stop; therefore, precautions were taken that they may not easily fall into this sin. They were said to have "played the harlot" (17:7), for idolatry was a breach of the covenant, just as adultery is a breach of the marriage covenant. It is in this context that God called Himself "a jealous God" (Exodus 20:5).

The main reason for such restrictions is to show Israel as different from the pagan nations; as holy unto the Lord God and acceptable to Him. This same holiness is required of believers today, though these Old Covenant ceremonial regulations gladly do not apply to us. Nonetheless, we may learn from their principles. Jesus is our altar; He is the true tabernacle (Hebrews 8:2), and to Him our sacrifices of praise are to be directed, and only through Him are our sacrifices acceptable to God. God demands that we go the the place He has prescribed and ordained. We find that place in Jesus.

A second strict law in chapter 17 stressed the prohibition of eating **blood** (17:10-14; cf. 3:17; 7:26). The reason was clearly stated: "the life of the flesh is in the blood" (17:11,14), but the main reason is that it was the means of atonement; it is the basis of the whole sacrificial system. Blood is vital to life, be it a human's or an animal's, and since life is sacred, blood had to be treated with respect (17:13; Genesis 9:5-6). Even one of the four rulings of the New Covenant church was to abstain from blood (Acts 15:29). The blood belongs to God, since He is the real life-giver. This fact ties into the first law given in this chapter (17:1-9). The blood of the sacrificed animal was to be brought to the prescribed place under the oversight of a priest (17:6). If this was disobeyed, the person was guilty of shedding blood wrongly and was given the severe penalty of being "cut off" (17:4), a reference to either death or exile. God used the blood to show mankind that it is only through the shedding of blood that remission for sin and communion with Him is made possible (Hebrews 9:14, 22).

Chapter 18 deals with the sacredness of people and relationships. We may wonder why some of these things (incest, 18:6-18; adultery, 18:20; homosexuality, 18:22; bestiality, 18:23; human sacrifice, 18:21) were even mentioned, but these were commonly practiced in the surrounding heathen nations, including Canaan. As the Lord's covenant people, the Israelites were to be drastically different from the heathen. Six times in chapter 18 they were warned against following their example (two times in verse 3, also in verses 24, 26, 27). They were to be pure and undefiled and to walk in the ways of the Lord, thus fulfilling their covenant obligation. God declared, "I am the Lord your God" (18:2) and as such He had the authority to make these commands. They were not given without a promise, for the one who followed them would "**live** by them". The Old Testament does not clarify what exactly this "living" entails, but the New Testament may shed some light on the meaning: abundant, full, true, and eternal life, found only through Christ's redemption and by following His ways.

Although the Old Covenant ceremonial laws no longer apply to us today, since they were fulfilled in Christ, the moral laws such as these still do. The "abominations" listed in this chapter are contrary to the ways of the Lord and to nature. The practice of such things leads to ruin and death (18:29). God hates these sins, but loves the sinner and desires to see him come to repentance that he may have life. But if one continues in sin, he will surely be punished, if not in this lifetime, then in the life hereafter with eternal death and hell-fire. The Canaanites and Amorites had not repented of their evil practices, thus their punishment was that they were to be vomited out of the land (18:24, 25,28; cf. Genesis 15:16) and replaced by the Israelites.

Prayer for today: *Lord God, please give us Your grace so that we may live in obedience to You, always doing those things that please You and not those things that displease You.*

Read Leviticus 19 *April 21*

Key Verse: Leviticus 19:18 *"... You shall love your neighbor as yourself: I am the Lord."*

This is a very important chapter among those dealing with the Law. This is evident by the Lord's command for Moses to tell these words to "all the congregation of the children of Israel." This is only the second time the Lord said these specific words; the first was with the instructions of the Passover (Exodus 12:3). Also, in verse two we are given the main reason for the precepts and the motivation for obedience: "You shall be holy, for I the Lord your God am holy". These laws are based on the fact of God's holiness which they were repeatedly told to exemplify.

This chapter emphasizes that the Lord (Yahweh) is the God of Israel. The phrase, "I am the Lord your God", occurs 15 times here. This is stressed to express His authority and to impress on the Israelites that they were His people and were to represent Him. They were also to clearly show other nations they were different and separated unto God. As such they were not to mix with other heathen nations (illustrated in 19:19), nor even be like them in the way they cut their hair and beards (19:27). They were forbidden participation in the common heathen practices of being tattooed, cutting themselves during a period of mourning (19:28), and prostitution which causes the land to be full of wickedness as well as breaking down the family unit.

Within this chapter, seven of the ten commandments are specifically reiterated: We find in verse 3, (1) honour your parents; and (2) keep the Sabbath. In verse 4 — (3) do not turn to idols (have no other gods before me); and (4) do not make "molded gods". In verse 11 we find (5) do not steal; (6) do not "deal falsely, nor lie"; and in verse 12 — (7) do not swear by God's name falsely, nor profane His name. There are also two other commandments implied throughout this chapter: in verse 18 — do not take vengeance, implying not to murder; and do not "bear any grudge", implying not to covet. The only one remaining is the commandment, "do not commit adultery", and it is thoroughly dealt with in the previous and following chapters. So we can see that these chapters have much to say to us today, for they concern morality, and these laws of God have never changed. The ten commandments are still valid for today.

What is the key to keeping the Lord commandments and keeping ourselves pure? Jesus answered this with His response to the question concerning the greatest commandment in the law. He quoted the last phrase of our key verse as the second greatest, the first being, "You shall love the Lord your God with all your heart, with all your soul, and with all your mind" (Matthew 22:36-39; cf. Deuteronomy 6:5). If one loves God with all his being, the natural outcome is obedience to Him (resulting in purity or holiness) and love for his neighbour. Jesus expressed that the long-range outcome of these two great commandments, which sum up all others, is eternal life (Luke 10:25-28). In this same conversation, Jesus was asked, "Who is my neighbour?" It is evident from His response with the parable of the Good Samaritan that a neighbour is defined as anyone with whom one comes in contact, not just those who live nearby (Luke 10:29-37). Jesus not only taught new things, but reflected the true spirit of the Old Covenant as well.

Jesus' Sermon on the Mount reflects much of what we read in Leviticus 19. God is concerned with the well-being of each individual in society, and we should be too, as well as being concerned about sharing the message of salvation. To care for the poor and the traveller, God commanded that the edges of the harvest and the gleanings remain for these needy people to gather (19:9,10; cf. Ruth 2:1-7). In this chapter, the people are encouraged to practise economic fairness (verse 13) and respect all people including the handicapped, senior citizens, and strangers (verse 14, 32, 33-34). There should be equal justice for all (verse 15), truthfulness and honesty in business affairs (verse 16, 35-36), and brotherly love for all, including the foreigner (verse 16-18, 34).

Prayer for today: *O Lord, we again ask for Your undeserved favour so that by Your power within us we can keep from doing wrong and keep doing right.*

Read Leviticus 20   *April 22*

Key Verse: Leviticus 20:26 *"And you shall be holy to Me for I the Lord am holy, and have separated you from the peoples, that you should be Mine."*

This chapter continues with the emphasis upon holiness and the Israelites' responsibility, as the covenant people, to remain separated from the heathen and obey the laws of God. Many laws found in the preceding two chapters are reiterated, but here we find the penalty involved with the various violations, and in many cases it was death. These punishments may seem harsh, but we have to remember the time period in which they were given and the type of people and customs of those days. Also, the Israelites had agreed to enter into a covenant relationship with God, whom they had made their sole sovereign, agreeing to follow Him with unquestioning obedience. They were, so to speak, under contract.

As we see in this chapter, God would not tolerate the worship of idols, witchcraft, the cursing of parents, nor any form of immorality. The penalties for these transgressions were described in very harsh ways such as: "put to death", "cut off", "stone him with stones", "burned with fire". Capital punishment reflects the extreme seriousness of the offense. All sin is a serious matter, but some were so abhorrent as to warrant immmediate death.

The worship of Molech, the god of the Ammonites, was accompanied by the detestable heathen practice of sacrificing children in the fire. This was revolting to God, and those Israelites guilty of this were to be stoned to death. If this was not done, God Himself would bring His judgment of death upon those who would "commit harlotry" (20:5). Overlooking such a terrible offense implied a certain sympathy toward it, and this would lead to the rapid breakdown of the whole covenant community. In fact, this is what history records to have happened later and it led to their downfall (Psalm 106:34-43; Jeremiah 7:30-31; 19:4; 32:31-36; Ezekiel 23:37).

Sin is described here as it actually is — something horrible which God abhors and which defiles Him, His sanctuary, and His name. It works like an infection and spreads to make uncleanliness in every place. Some of the words used to describe the various offenses reflect the seriousness of sin: "harlotry" (verse 5), "perversion" (verse 12), "abomination" (verse 13), "wickedness" (verse 14), "disgrace" and "guilt" (N.I.V., verse 17), "an unclean thing" or "an act of impurity" (verse 21). The Bible does not try to cover up the horribleness of sin, rather it exposes it for what it is. The holiness of God is what we must attain, and that brings sin out into the open. We sometimes find people today, sadly even some believers, trying to put a sugar coating over something that is actually poison. Sin is sin, and no less. God sees every sin, and for the unrepentant there will indeed come punishment, whether in this life or the next. But thanks be to God for His great grace, for even the sins that deserve death can be forgiven because of the work Jesus wrought on the cross in bearing them away.

The regulations of the covenant were not meant to bring hardship to those God called His own, but rather joy and peace with Him and with the community of faith. Such laws and penalties, however, were necessary to guide the people in the ways of holiness, as well as serving to warn and deter potential offenders. Being God's elect today also has many serious responsibilities, as well as many privileges. In the teachings of the New Covenant, separation from worldliness and following the way of holiness are still expected of those God calls His own. Like the Old Covenant, we find holiness is still clearly defined in following and obeying the Lord. Although it is a narrow and difficult path (Matthew 7:13-14), by God's grace, it is not impossible. We are exhorted to "pursue...holiness, without which no one will see the Lord" (Hebrews 12:14).

Prayer for today: *O Holy God, by faith we join those around Your throne who worship You saying, "Holy, holy, holy". Enable us to walk in the light of Your holiness, not in an attitude toward others of "Holier than thou", but in humility as sinners who are forgiven because we've asked You and You promised You'd do it.*

Read Leviticus 21 & 22   *April 23*

Key Verse: Leviticus 22:32 *"You shall not profane My holy name, but I will be hallowed among the children of Israel. I am the Lord who sanctifies you."*

In the preceding chapters, we have seen the standards of holiness for the common Israelite. In these two chapters, we see the standards of holiness required for the priesthood. These are naturally high standards because of their position of responsibility, for "everyone to whom much is given, from him much will be required" (Luke 12:48). Whatever is to be done must be done in light of the holiness and perfection of God; therefore, the priest had to maintain a holy, pure, and exemplary life, so that he could then lead and teach the children of Israel the ways of holiness and how to truly hallow God's holy name.

In their service to God at the tabernacle, the priests were to remain pure at all times. They were forbidden to touch any dead body and thereby defile themselves (since death is the result of sin), although exceptions were made in the case of a very close relative for whom the priest was responsible. Under no conditions was any priest to mourn for the dead in the manner of the heathen (21:5,10). The rules regarding cleanness for the high priest were even more strict than for the other priests. He was never, under any circumstances, to go near a dead body which would then defile him, for he wore the holy garments and the consecrating anointing oil of God was upon him (21:12). He was to openly express no sadness or mourning, but be ready for the joyous service of God at all times. He, as all priests, was only to marry a godly, noble, virgin Israelite (21:7,13-14), and his behaviour was to be exemplary in all areas, for he was the people's representative to God and God's representative to the people.

The priests stood in a special place and were to exemplify the holiness of God by separating themselves from any defilement or evil. If any priest transgressed, it was very serious and the penalties were far more severe than for the rest of the people, since they had greater responsibility and were expected to know better. The priests' families were also to be above reproach and live holy lives, for if not, they would bring extreme disgrace upon him (21:9). In the eastern culture, the family ties were (and still are) very close, so that whatever one member does effects the whole family in a personal way.

The priests and the sacrificial animals which atoned for sin were to picture, or typify, the perfect High Priest, Jesus Christ. Therefore, those priests who offered the holy things were to have no blemish or deformity (21:17). In God's service at the tabernacle, everything involved was to display perfection and thus be glorifying unto Him, for anything short of perfection profanes His holiness. This regulation was another of the many external signs to show that it is a serious thing to approach God and was not to be taken lightly. God is holy, therefore His servants alike were to be holy and symbolize His holiness.

Believers today, as Christ's priesthood, are to have the same exemplary holy life that was expected of the Old Covenant priests. As the Apostle Paul exhorted: "We give no offense in anything, that our ministry may not be blamed. But in all things we commend ourselves as ministers of God:...by purity, by knowledge, by longsuffering, by kindness, by the Holy Spirit, by sincere love, by the word of truth, by the power of God, by the armour of righteousness..." (2 Corinthians 6:3-4a, 6-7). The sanctifying work of the Holy Spirit is desperately needed that we may live pure and holy lives in this unclean and defiled world.

Prayer for today: *O Lord, we pray for our spiritual leaders. Grant to them the grace of purity so that their example will be excellent and so that they can say as Paul said, "Follow me as I follow Christ."*

Read Leviticus 23   April 24

Key Verse: Leviticus 23:2 "...*The feasts of the Lord, which you shall proclaim to be holy convocations, these are My feasts.*"

Thus far in the book of Leviticus, we have learned about the holiness of the sanctuary and the sacrifices as well as the holiness of the people and the priests; now we come to the chapter dealing with the "holy convocations" which are the "feasts of the Lord" (23:2,37). The complete calendar of the Israelite religious year is briefly described here. The celebrations were designed to remind the people that all good gifts, such as a good harvest, come from God and are manifestations of His care, love and goodness. Observing these feasts at the proper times and in the prescribed manner showed their obedience and loyalty to God. These feasts also served to remind Israel, especially to the coming generations, of the great things God had done for them.

The most important and the oldest feast God designated was the weekly observance of the **Sabbath** (23:3), their day of rest. It reminded them of His creative work (Genesis 1-2:3; Exodus 31:17) and was a sign of their covenant relationship (Exodus 31:13) and His redeeming them from bondage (Deuteronomy 5:15). It was the Lord's "holy day", a "pleasure", "delight", and "honourable" day (Isaiah 58:13). Although the stress is upon physical rest and refreshment, the primary purpose was spiritual refreshment in renewing fellowship with God.

The **Passover** (23:4-5) marked the beginning of the religious year. It began at sunset on the fourteenth day of the first month called "Nisan" (March or April). It was a lunar calendar, so the months vary from year to year. The first passover was observed in Egypt (Exodus 12:2,6-7,12). In this very significant feast, the Israelites proclaimed the redeeming grace of God and reaffirmed their faith in Him. It was to always remind them of God's miraculous intervention on their behalf in Egypt when the Lord's death angel "passed over" the homes with the blood applied to its doorposts. Likewise, the Last Supper reminds us today of Jesus' intervention and sacrificial blood that was shed to be applied to the doorposts of our hearts.

The Feast of **Unleavened Bread** (fifteenth of Nisan) accompanied the celebrations of the Passover. For a period of seven days, the first and seventh being sabbaths, the Israelites were to eat only unleavened bread and all the men were required to be present before the Lord (Deuteronomy 16:16). It commemorated their exodus from slavery, for they were to take only unleavened bread (Exodus 12:39) and leave immediately at the time when God opened the way because of His many miracles, the climax of which was the Passover. Believers are to "purge out the old leaven [sin]..." and be "...unleavened. For indeed Christ, our Passover, was sacrificed for us" (1 Corinthians 5:7).

When the people entered the Promised Land, they were to observe the Feast of **First Fruits**. This occured when the first early crop was ready for harvest, sometime in April. No grain from the new crop was to be eaten until they acknowledged that it had come as a blessing from God. Jesus Christ is called "the first fruits of those who have fallen asleep" (1 Corinthians 15:20-23). Just as the first ripe grain came as a promise of more harvest to follow, so Christ's resurrection assures us of the coming spiritual harvest and our own future resurrection.

The Feast of **Pentecost**, meaning "fiftieth [day]", also called the Feast of Weeks, is a sabbath celebration coming 50 days after the start of the First Fruits. It was the second feast for which all Israelite males were to be in attendance. It was a joyous occasion in thankfulness to the Lord for the harvest and for providing their daily bread. They were not to forget the needy, so they were reminded to leave the gleanings (23:22).

The Feast of **Trumpets** was a holy Sabbath on the first day of the seventh month of Tishri (October). The people would blow the ram's horn to awaken Israel to prepare for the important and most solemn **Day of Atonement** which came ten days later. This was observed by a sabbath, a fast, and the sacrifice of animals to atone for sin. Even though there were many sacrifices through the year, this was not sufficient to cover sin. This serious day reminded the Israelites that there could be no joy in their covenant relationship without sin being dealt with, especially through the substitute (details in Leviticus 16).

On the fifteenth day of the same month of Tishri, the Feast of **Tabernacles** began and lasted for eight days. The first and eighth days were holy Sabbaths and, for the third time in the year, all the men were to appear before the Lord. During this time, the Israelites lived in booths to remind them of God's provision and protection after their departure from Egypt and their travelling in the wilderness, living in crude tents and booths. It confirmed their acknowledgement that the Lord, Yahweh, was their God (23:43).

Prayer for today: *Lord God, You have given us a great weekly convocation in the New Covenant called "The Lord's Day". Grant us the grace to be obedient so we will not forsake the assembling of ourselves together (Hebrew 10:25).*

Read Leviticus 24 *April 25*

Key Verse: Leviticus 24:22 *"You shall have the same law for the stranger and for one from your own country; for I am the Lord your God."*

This chapter speaks about the holy light, the holy bread, and the Holy Name. The finest and most pure olive oil was to be provided by the people so that Aaron, and all the succeeding high priests might "make the lamps burn continually" (24:2; cf. Exodus 25:31-40). This golden lampstand found in the Holy Place was the only source of light in the tabernacle. The light represents Jesus Christ, the only true light of the world (John 8:12). The holy oil in the Bible typically represents the Holy Spirit. It was important for the lampstand to be continually attended to, to keep a fresh and full supply of oil burning. Similarly, it is necessary that believers keep their lives full of the Holy Spirit, that Jesus' light may shine brightly.

Also found in the Holy Place was the pure gold table of showbread (Exodus 25:23-30). This was replenished every Sabbath with twelve large fresh loaves of bread which Aaron and his sons were to eat in the Holy Place. These loaves signified God's sustenance and provision for His people and may have represented the twelve tribes of Israel. Jesus called Himself "the bread of life", for whoever comes unto Him will never hunger (John 6:35). Spiritual food is necessary for our souls, just as physical food is necessary for the body.

To illustrate the holiness of the Name of God, and to describe the seriousness of blasphemy against the Lord, this incident is recorded: a man, while fighting, was caught cursing the name of God. Since up until this point no penalty had been given for breaking this third commandment, the man was confined until Moses heard from the Lord what he should do. The severe punishment of stoning to death was the answer, for the offender was to bear his own guilt. The witnesses, by putting their hands on his head, represented his own responsibility for what was to befall him. It served as a lesson for everyone to be aware of the seriousness of blasphemy or even taking the name of God lightly. The Lord God was to be honoured by all and His Holy Name revered and feared, even by foreigners living among the covenant people (24:22; Exodus 12:49), for His laws are universal and His judgments just.

As well as capital punishment for blasphemy, we find here the same punishment also restated for premeditated murder; this punishment had been instituted by God much earlier (Genesis 9:6). In general, the main principle of the civil law was retribution. In this way, it limited retaliation or revenge for the wrong committed. For example, if one's eye was put out he, or a family member, might want to kill the guilty person, but this law prevented such revenge and permitted only an equal punishment, the putting out of the guilty person's eye. (24:20) For the Israelites, who were to administer the punishment publicly, this would be just and fair, for the penalty was to fit the crime and not exceed it.

Jesus did not change or abolish the law, nor did He deny the exercise of civil law, but He modified and brought a new light on it. Concerning retribution He said to turn the other cheek, "love your enemies, do good to those who hate you" (Luke 6:28-29). Jesus' teaching brought a fuller revelation of truth. Concerning capital punishment for such things as breaking the Sabbath and adultery, He showed that He had all authority, for He was the "Lord of the Sabbath" (Mark 2:28), and He displayed mercy and grace to the woman caught in adultery. He looked upon the heart, rather than the actions. To do good on the sabbath (as Jesus did and was accused, John 5:15-16) was in keeping with the spirit of the Sabbath. He internalized the law. In the case of the woman caught in adultery, Jesus stirred the crowd's conscience. Everyone had sin and therefore had no right to throw the first stone. Jesus did not condemn her, rather, in mercy, He gave her the opportunity for repentance (John 8:3-11). Because of sin, we all deserve death, but because of the marvelous work of Jesus and His intercession, we no longer live under the curse of the Law, but under God's wonderful grace (Galatians 3:13; Romans 6:15).

Prayer for today: O great God and Father of our Lord Jesus Christ, grant that the windows of our lives will always be clear to receive Your light of truth. May we ever feast on Your Show Bread, Jesus, and help us to lift up in reverence the Name which is above every Name, the Name of Jesus.

Read Leviticus 25　　　*April 26*

Key Verse: Leviticus 25:10a *"And you shall consecrate the fiftieth year, and proclaim liberty throughout all the land to all its inhabitants."*

This chapter is related to Leviticus 23 in giving regulations concerning the consecrated times of year. It extends the principle of the sabbath, as one day in seven, to a sabbath rest of the land every seventh year, and an additional sabbath on the fiftieth or Jubilee year. During these years no land was to be cultivated in any manner, meaning there was to be no sowing, reaping, pruning of vines, or gathering of fruit. God, in His great wisdom, saw to it that the land had one year in every seven, and two years in a row every forty-ninth and fiftieth year, that it might be replenished and regain optimum fertility.

This legislation is an excellent agricultural and ecological practice in the conservation of natural resources. All the land is the Lord's, and He who is its creator knows what is best for it. This practice makes it clear to the Israelites that God is the owner of the land, and in a sense they are but tenants who were to follow His instructions concerning His land (25:23). If they would observe these years as God legislated, He would grant them the conditional promises: "you will dwell in the land in safety" (25:18), "the land will yield its fruit" and "you will eat your fill" (25:19), and finally, He promised to bless them in the sixth year with great abundance so they would have plenty for the seventh and even more than enough for the year of Jubilee (25:21).

As well as these years providing a rest for the land, they were also years when all debts among fellow Israelites were to be cancelled and all Hebrew slaves to be freed (Deuteronomy 15:1-15). The basic theme for these years of rest is liberation for that which was bound. The year of Jubilee was announced by joyous and loud trumpet blasts from the ram's horn every fiftieth year at the close of Day of Atonement. At this point, they had just received divine freedom from their sin, and so it was a time to rejoice. They were to "proclaim liberty throughout all the land" (25:10). It was to remind them that they had once been slaves in Egypt, but God had miraculously set them free and redeemed them. With the agreement of entering into the covenant relationship with Him, they now became bound to God and only free to serve Him. Also, in the year of Jubilee, all land that had been sold during the course of the previous fifty years was to be returned to the original owner of inheritance (25:10). By this they were to learn that spiritual wealth and obedience to God was more important than material possessions.

These years may be said to symbolize the spiritual rest and liberation from the power of sin which all believers receive when they come to Jesus Christ (John 8:35-36; Galatians 5:1). They are enabled and encouraged to learn to live by faith, depending totally upon God (Galatians 2:20). A year free from responsibilities of the usual toil was not meant to make them lazy, but to give them opportunity to devote more time to the Lord, learning His law and trusting in Him.

Observing these years would teach them to be generous and not forget the needs of the poverty stricken, but to share in the bounty of God's blessings. Whatever grew of its own accord was not to be gathered in the usual manner. No one in particular was to put any claim on it, but all were free to eat that which went from hand to mouth. In such a way it served as provision for the poor, the servants and the strangers in the land (25:5-7). We also find here a practical application of loving one's neighbour as oneself, for within the covenant community, no one was allowed to go hungry and those who were able were to lend to the poor without charging any interest (25:35-36).

This, as well as the legislation demanding proper treatment of slaves, would ensure that the poor were not exploited, but rather treated with human dignity (25:43).

We were once enslaved to sin, but Jesus has become our kinsman redeemer who does a better work than those friends who paid the price to redeem their kin from bondage (25:48-49). He paid with His very life to redeem us. Jesus may have referred to that year in His explanation of the purpose for His coming. He brings true liberty to the oppressed and teaches the true meaning of the "acceptable year of the Lord" (Luke 4:18-19, 21).

Prayer for today: Lord, Your truth is that "Now is the accepted time, now is the day of salvation." Help us by the power of Jesus' Name today and every day to proclaim deliverance to the captives and to set at liberty them that are bruised.

Read Leviticus 26 *April 27*

Key Verse: Leviticus 26:40,42 *"But if they confess their iniquity... then I will remember My covenant with Jacob,...Isaac and... Abraham..."*

In this chapter of magnificent promises and terrible warnings, the Lord God stresses two basic and important requirements that demanded obedience. Firstly, the second commandment is written, forbidding the making and worshipping of idols, or any carved images. The Lord God is a jealous God and will not share His glory (Isaiah 42:8). Secondly, they were to be careful to observe the fourth commandment of keeping the Sabbaths holy, meaning not only the day, but the Sabbath year, and the Sabbath Jubilee (Leviticus 25), as well as honouring and showing reverence for God's holy sanctuary. If these were kept as God required, the other commandments would flow naturally, resulting in His granting the many beautiful blessings. But all these are conditional; the blessings for obedience (26:3), and the curses for disobedience (26:14).

The Lord God spoke clearly: "If you walk in My statutes and keep My commandments, and perform them" (26:3), then the results would be wonderful. He promised material blessings of rain, abundant harvests, much food, and much offspring (26:4-5, 9-10), peace, security, protection, victory over enemies (26:6-8), and, most importantly, spiritual blessings — His presence among them, for they would be His people (26:11-12). As with the passages of law, these verses are followed by God's solemn words which serve to remind them of their covenant and obligation of obedience to Him: "I am the Lord your God" (26:13).

The total opposite of blessings, namely curses, would result if they were disobedient. Again the Lord speaks clearly and graphically: "If you despise My statutes" and "do not perform all My commandments, but break My covenant" (26:15), then He would bring terrible calamities upon them. If these first few punishments (26:16-17) did not bring about repentance and obedience to Him, then four times God says, "I will punish you seven times more for your sins" (26:18, 21, 24, 28). After each time, the punishments would become successively more severe. This is because, in His great love, God desired to see them come to repentance, but until then their punishment would be sickness, defeat and famine; then, after the fourth and final warning, the worst possible punishment would result: to be scattered among the heathen nations in captivity where many would perish, and their land would lie desolate (26:29-35). We find that all these things happened in the course of Israel's history (e.g. Ezekiel 14:21), for sadly, they did not keep the covenant with their God. Along with the privileges of the covenant came responsibility and duty. These severe punishments were a result of the holy and just character of God, who cannot stand sin nor tolerate disobedience, especially among His covenant people. In times of obedience to God, His holy presence dwelt among them, but because He could not dwell with sinfulness, He would have to turn His face from them (26:17). We find in this chapter more spoken of curses than blessings, for the people were to fully understand the seriousness of God's commands and their covenant obligations.

However, the Lord promised that if the Israelites would confess their iniquity with humble hearts, He would remember the covenant with their forefathers (26:40,42; key verse; c.f. 1 Chronicles 7;14). Notice the reason given is not because of them, but because of the eternal covenant with Abraham, and God's word does not change. The covenant of Sinai was conditional, but the covenant with Abraham was one of grace, never to be nullified. Therefore God, in His love and mercy, said He would not totally destroy them all, but would leave a remnant, those few faithful ones. May we today be those faithful ones who follow in the ways of the Lord and, though undeserving, receive His promised blessings provided through Jesus Christ.

Prayer for today: Grant today, O God of Grace, that we will be enabled to love You with all our hearts, minds, souls and strengths, and to love our neighbours as ourselves. Help us mightily because in keeping these, we also keep the whole law.

Read Leviticus 27 *April 28*

Key Verse: Leviticus 27:30 *"And all the tithe of the land,...is the Lord's. It is holy to the Lord."*

This final chapter of Leviticus deals with vows of consecrated things, vows of devoted things, and tithes unto the Lord. The things vowed or solemnly promised to the Lord were not made as a requirement of obedience to any law, but given voluntarily out of devotion and thanksgiving to God.

A person could consecrate unto the Lord things he owned, such as animals, houses, fields, or even himself and people for whom he was responsible. The priest would estimate the value and the person would donate to the sanctuary the money it was found to be worth. A poor person could still have this privilege, because the priest made the valuation according to his ability (27:8). There was a certain price for people according to their ages and sex. Males were worth more than females, probably because of being physically stronger. The highest valuation was put upon those in the prime of life (between ages twenty to sixty), for they were more able and therefore obliged to do more in the service of the Lord.

Houses and fields could be dedicated to the Lord as well. It seems that a house would be given over to the priests to be sold and the proceeds given to the Lord's work. Only part of a field of one's possession (land alotted to his family from the first division of Canaan) could be dedicated to God (27:16), for the Lord did not want to see an over-zealous person cause the ruin of his whole family. The value of the field was estimated according to the cost to plant it until the next year of Jubilee (27:17-18), when the law required it to be returned to the original family (27:21).

The law was flexible and humane, for under certain conditions it allowed for the discharge of a vow of something consecrated unto the Lord. The consecrated thing could be redeemed, or bought back, by paying the price it was valued at plus an additional twenty percent penalty. This penalty would serve as an extra caution to encourage only serious vows and to protect the sanctity of the vow, for once a solemn vow was made before witnesses, great care was to be taken that it be kept. In the New Testament, there are no such stipulations concerning vows made to God; however, it is made clear that a promise to God is a serious thing which is expected to be honoured, be it the consecrating of oneself to God, or a baptismal or marriage vow.

It appears that under a different type of vow, a person could "devote" things to God (27:28). The Hebrew word means the irrevocable giving over of something to the Lord. In such instances, it became most holy and wholly the Lord's. Verse 29 is somewhat unclear, but there seems to be a difference between things devoted and things "under the ban", which are doomed or "devoted to destruction" (N.I.V.). The Hebrew meaning implies the irrevocable giving over of a person or thing to the Lord by totally destroying them. It seems most probable that the ban came as a result of the Lord's direct instructions, or the decision of all the congregation or elders of Israel, like the destruction of their enemies (e.g. the city of Jericho, Joshua 6:17; the Amalekekites, 1 Samuel 15:22-3).

Finally, before the book of Leviticus closes, the Israelites were reminded that "all the tithe of the land" belonged to the Lord (27:30) and was to be brought to the priests. To refuse to pay the tithe was, and still is, robbing God (Malachi 3:8). There were various kinds of tithes, but here we see stressed the tithe of the produce of the land. Since God is the true owner (Leviticus 25:23), it is regarded as His due offering, expressing thanks for all His blessings. Believers today should not give any less to God than those in the Old Covenant. We also are to honour the Lord with our possessions (Proverbs 3:9) and give our tithes and offerings where we receive spiritual food so that the Lord's ministers may be supported, and to aid in the spread of the gospel of Jesus Christ (1 Corinthians 9:11,14; 16:2; Galatians 6:6,10).

Prayer for today: *Almighty God, we give ourselves to You. Keep us faithful in giving back to You that minimum which we owe, the tithe, and also help us to be liberal and generous givers of offerings over and above our tithes.*

Luke

Luke is the only Gentile writer in the New Testament. He is also the most prolific. His two-volume work, Luke and Acts, is larger than even Paul's combined epistles. He was from Alexandria in Northern Africa, and was a physician by profession. The only one of the Gospel writers never to have seen Jesus in the flesh, he writes as a time historian. His intended audience is Greek. Thus he omits much of the Semitic and Latin references wherever possible. For instance the words "Iscariot", "Abba", "hosanna", "Gethsemane", and "Golgatha" are not used. Nor do we find "Talitha cumi" or "Eloi, Eloi, lama sabachthani". "Rabbi" is usually rendered "master" or "lord".

Luke's purpose was to inform a high official by the name of Theophilus about Jesus and the new Jewish/Gentile sect known as Christianity. He does so with a scrupulous commitment to what is called "primary research". That is, his work is the result of strenuous hours of conducting personal interviews with those who walked and talked with Jesus.

Among other things, Luke wanted to show that Christianity was not a subversive sect. He also wanted to highlight the work of the Spirit. Whereas Mark makes six references to the Spirit, and Matthew twelve, Luke refers to the Spirit seventeen times in his Gospel, and fifty-seven times in the book of Acts. He also emphasizes the prayer life of Jesus and the vital place of prayer in the life of the early church. He stresses the role of women in the history of the church. Of no less importance is his emphasis on the post-resurrection appearances of Jesus.

What makes Luke's writings so special, however, is the already-stated fact of his being an historian. Christianity after all, is not rooted in mystery, but in history. Whether we accept Jesus or not, Luke tells us He lived, died, and rose again, and ascended *in history*. Our history.

Read Luke 1 & 2 *April 29*

Key Verse: Luke 2:30,32 *"My eyes have seen Your salvation...a light to bring revelation to the Gentiles, and the glory of Your people Israel."*

I'm a Gentile; a Gentile who, with his family, lived among Jewish friends and neighbours for seven years in Jerusalem. We speak Hebrew (Kathy and the children, fluently — I, not so fluently), and we have an intimate knowledge of, and great respect for, Jewish culture and religion. In fact, even after being back in Canada this past year and a half, our kids still feel more Israeli than Canadian.

Friends and acquaintances here have often remarked, "It must have been wonderful to live in the Holy Land! Especially at Christmas and Easter!" Well, yes it was — but not for the reasons you'd expect. Christmas is basically a non-event, at least in terms of the Israeli calendar. There are special events in "Manger Square" on Christmas Eve in Bethlehem, but in Jerusalem, Tel Aviv, Haifa, and all places in between, Christmas day is just like any other day. At Easter you'll see groups of Roman Catholic or Orthodox pilgrims carrying life-like crosses along the Via Dolorosa in the Old City, and Protestant groups holding a sunrise service at the Garden Tomb, but again, for Israelis, generally, it's just another day. That's the irony of Christian celebrations in Israel — her most famous son is remembered not by His own but by the "Goyim", the Gentiles from the "outside". Right now, Jesus is anything but "the glory of Your people Israel".

But He is "revelation to the Gentiles". Which suggests that Simeon, as he held the eight-day-old infant Jesus, spoke prophetically. The notion that Jesus would be a revelation to the Gentiles was definitely novel, and undoubtedly future. That future, however, is now — we Gentiles have received the message. And Israel has yet to embrace the baby. So, even as I write these words and you read them, we're living in an historically dynamic tension between the "time of the Gentiles" and the day when Israel will recognize her Messiah. What a day that will be! And it may be soon. Simeon's words will be fulfilled.

Prayer for Today: *Thank You Lord for the Light to bring revelation to us as we are Gentiles. May we let our light shine to all others including Your people Israel.*

Read Luke 3 *April 30*

John the Baptist must have seemed a rather arrogant fellow to some — how may preachers do you know who address candidates for baptism as a "brood of vipers"? He was so opposite the typical evangelist/prophet with their promotional schemes and follow-up plans. In fact, when people (multitudes of them) showed up for his baptismal ministry, he seemed surprised that they'd come at all — "who warned you to flee from the coming wrath?" Nor was he above knocking religious and national heritage, "Do not begin to say to yourselves, 'We have Abraham as our father'. For I tell you that out of these stones God can raise up children for Abraham." Imagine some preacher assessing your worth as roughly equivalent to a stone! He seemed to many to be an obnoxious man with an offensive message.

The whole point of John's baptism was, "repentance for the forgiveness of sins". Notice it wasn't "confession" for the forgiveness of sins. Without question, confession is vital to the redemptive process, but confession is relatively passive; once you've confessed, then what? Confess again? And again? Repentance, on the other hand, is active. What's more, it's creative.

For example, how's this for active and creative: "The man with two tunics should share with him who has none, and the one who has food should do the same..." To tax collectors, he says, "Don't collect any more than you are required to." To occupying soldiers, he says, "Don't extort money...don't accuse people falsely...be content with your pay." This is the fruit worthy of repentance.

Repentance means turning away from a sinful choice and choosing or walking in the opposite direction. Yes, we must confess our sin — that's step number one. But then comes the arduous and sometimes life-long challenge of choosing the new direction and the new values — every day until the day we enter His presence.

Prayer for Today: *Lord God, we thank You for the privilege of confessing our sins and for Your promise of forgiveness. Help us to repent so that the "Fruit" — love, joy, peace, longsuffering, kindness, goodness, faithfulness, gentleness and self control, will show to You and others that we are repentant people.*

MAY

"The Shepherd's Field" — Bethlehem

Special Note: Be sure to write in your request by JUNE 1 for your next volume of *DAY UNTO DAY, Year One – Summer* edition. It starts July 1!

Read Luke 4   *May 1*

Key Verse: Luke 4:24 *"...no prophet is accepted in his own country"*.

You've heard the old adage, "familiarity breeds contempt". And if not contempt, familiarity breeds at least neglect. This was the case with Jesus. Interestingly, it was also the case with the nation of Israel. And, if we're honest, it's the case with you and me too.

In Luke's account, the temptation in the wilderness is followed by Jesus' return to Nazareth, His home town. There He attends the synagogue on the Sabbath, and when it's His turn to read, He finds Isaiah 61. After reading verses 1 and 2, He looks at the assembled men of Nazareth, all friends and acquaintances, and says, "Today this scripture is fulfilled in your hearing." This obviously met with resistance, for Jesus goes on to say, "no prophet is accepted in his home town" (NIV). Then, as the anger of the home town men mounts, Jesus does nothing to diffuse it, rather He adds fuel to the fire.

He goes on to refer to Elijah and Elisha's time. Prophets then were no more listened to by their own people than now, Jesus says in effect. During the three-and-a-half year drought, there were probably thousands of Israelite widows in need. But what does God do? He sends Elijah to a Canaanite woman, a heathen. During Elisha's day, there were many sick with leprosy. But whom does God heal? Not an Israelite, but a Syrian. The implication was clear, and not lost on Jesus' audience. So much so that they tried to throw Him over a cliff.

The people of God are often those least accessible to Him. We're often in church, often praying, often talking about God. We're very religious. In fact, religion is old hat. And that familiarity produces carelessness, boredom and neglect.

It needn't do so. Not if we thank God every day of our lives for His wonderful gift of life in Jesus Christ. Not if we renew our love every morning, live it all day, and rest in it at night. You might call it "familiar freshness".

Prayer for Today: Lord Jesus, in this reading You have revealed Yourself as the One who preached the Gospel, healed the broken hearted, set at liberty the captives and met all human need. Thank You for meeting our needs, and grant that today we will have Your strength to share this good news with others.

Read Luke 5 *May 2*

Key Verse: Luke 5:38 *"...new wine must be put into new wineskins..."*

Let's follow Jesus' thinking here. New wine needs new wineskins — that makes sense. Old wineskins have already been stretched by the fermentation process. Stretch them any more and they'll burst. So the old wineskins are useless now; they've served their purpose. But does that mean the old wine is useless? By no means. In Jesus' own words, "the old is better". Let's pursue this a bit.

You've heard the term, "the old boys network". I remember, as a young pastor, attending church conferences and seeing the old boys network in effect. A church would be in distinct need of a pastor — in my mind, it needed a young, fresh, new approach: someone in tune with the time. But what would the district officials do? They'd appoint one of the "old boys", a friend of long acquaintance, to go in and continue the old traditions, stultifying the church even more. My young pastor friends and I would shake our heads with not-so-muted disdain. The status quo seemed to be preferred to creatively pursuing the far horizon. The district officials chose men from the ark, while we younger pastors wanted someone from the cradle. We wanted style, they wanted character.

I see things more clearly, now that I've reached the hoary-headed age of 42. The brand new church needs a young pastor — while the young leader "ferments", the church expands, relatively painlessly. On the other hand, if the young pastor is catapulted into an established situation, chances are there'll be an explosion (not of growth, but of disintegration). The seasoned pastor, on the other hand, is the man to cultivate, prime, nourish, discipline, and guide the seasoned church in producing ongoing fruit. Of course, there are exceptions, but generally speaking, whereas character always has style, style doesn't always have character.

Jesus' teaching was new. The established religious system couldn't bear the pressure of His expansive view of the kingdom of heaven; something had to give. But even while the establishment crushed Jesus' life, His shed blood, like the released juice of the grape, created a whole new wine. And ultimately, it was the old wineskin that burst — and a new world, which will culminate in Jesus' return, was begun.

But there's something unique about Jesus' new wine. It's rooted in the old. It has the style of a new day dawning, and the character of Abraham, Isaac, and Jacob. It's the best of new and old.

Prayer for Today: *Lord Jesus, in You we are a new creation. Your life in us is the new wine of Your kingdom. Help us to share You with others today.*

Read Luke 6 *May 3*

Key Verse: Luke 6:47 *"Whoever comes to Me... hears My sayings and does them..."*

Verbal Christianity can be quite enjoyable. You talk about love, discuss theology, give to the poor at Christmas, get lots of "amens!" when speaking about faith to the converted — in fact, it beats most other service clubs all hollow. Mainly because a "Christian" club brings an abundance of self-satisfying righteousness as part of the territory. Your club dues are paid in right talking.

Right walking, rather than talking, is, of course, what Christianity is about. Especially in the 90's. There are enough talking heads out there; it's time for walking feet. Jesus thought so, then. No doubt, He still thinks so today.

He said there was a distinct relationship between hearing (and "parroting", I'd expect) His sayings, and doing them. In fact, He used a powerful simile to make the point. The person who is a hearer and a talker without being a doer, is like someone building a house on an unstable foundation. Regardless of the dedication, the diligence and the time spent in construction, the house will collapse. It doesn't even matter if the house was dedicated to the Lord's work. If the foundation is shaky, the house will be shaky, and ultimately will be no more.

Conversely, the person who not only hears, but also puts Jesus' words into practise, builds an indestructible house. Regardless of the forces that come against it, the house will stand. Why? Because "doing" the word makes for an unshakable foundation. Perhaps no more or less effort will be put into the construction than the house built on sand, but the house on the Rock will stand forever.

In the final analysis, our talk doesn't impress God. He can make the rocks cry out if He wants to — so spare yourself and Him all the talk; rather, give Him your will. Get out of that pew, and do!

Prayer for Today: *Lord Jesus, grant us Your power to walk our talk. During the last few days, O Lord, we've asked You to help us to witness of You. Now Lord help us to do a kindness today to those to whom we've witnessed.*

Read Luke 7 *May 4*

Key Verse: Luke 7:9 "... *I say to you, I have not found such great faith, not even in Israel!*"

Most everyone likes to know what others think of them. And, if it were possible, to know what God thinks of them. What most of us know, however, is what we think of ourselves. Generally, when it comes to self-assessment, we're not too impressed with what we see.

The centurion in this chapter certainly wasn't stuck on himself. In fact, he didn't even consider himself worthy to come to Jesus to request healing for his servant. Instead, he cleverly sent some of the Jewish elders of Capernaum to present his case to Jesus. These elders had a high view of the centurion — "he loves our nation and has built our synagogue," they said. So Jesus went with them to the centurion's house.

But, before He reached the house, some friends of the centurion came to meet Jesus with this message, "Don't bother yourself with the walk over here. Just say the word and my servant will be healed. After all, my commands are obeyed by my men — why shouldn't your command be obeyed by the sickness?" Jesus was impressed; so much so that He said, "I have not found such great faith, even in Israel." This Gentile was putting Jesus' nation to shame in terms of his faith. His friends returned to the house and found the servant healed.

So, the centurion was rather self-deprecating in his view of himself. The elders, on the other hand, were very high on him. And Jesus was impressed with his faith. The point? Simply that your self-assessment may not be entirely accurate. There's something to be said for giving yourself the benefit of the doubt. After all, God loves you. And He's a pretty good judge of what's truly valuable.

Prayer for Today: *Lord Jesus in today's reading You spoke the Word to John the Baptist, telling him that You made the blind see and did many other miracles. May we take You at Your Word as the centurion did and expect miracles according to Your Word.*

Read Luke 8 *May 5*

Key Verse: Luke 8:15 "*But the ones that fell on the good ground are those who, having heard the word with a noble and good heart, keep it and bear fruit with patience.*"

Hear. Retain. Produce. That's what "noble and good hearts" do. The object of the hearing and retaining is the Word of God (v.11). And "fruit" is the result.

What kind of fruit? Well, Jesus doesn't say. What He *does* say is that the fruit produced represents "a hundred times more than was sown" (v. 8). We're talking a 10,000 percent increase here! Pretty intimidating. Especially if we think of a single seed as one soul won to Christ. Is Jesus suggesting we're to reproduce ourselves 100 times? What about those of us who've won maybe one or two people to the Lord in our entire lives? What about those who've yet to lead their *first* soul to Christ?

Before you're overcome with a performance-anxiety attack, let's think it through. Fruitfulness in the Bible is never described only in soul-winning terms. In fact, the apostle Paul talks of it in terms of "love, joy, peace, longsuffering, kindness, goodness, faithfulness, gentleness, self-control...", the "fruit of the Spirit" (Gal.5:22,23). Fruit, then, refers to the general quality, as well as the quantity, of your life. If we're producing peace, joy or goodness among our neighbours, we're fruitful. If we're leading a neighbour or two to the Lord, as well, then that's fruitfulness, too. Indeed, if we're bringing our heavenly Father some joy, I daresay that's fruitfulness as well.

The key is to be fruitful rather than parasitical. Be an extension of God's love for the world. Do this, and you'll be one of those with "a noble and good heart".

Prayer For Today: *Lord God, Your Word says, "He that winneth souls is wise." Please grant us Your wisdom in translating Your life and character into the language which our family, neighbours and friends will understand. Amen!*

Read Luke 9   *May 6*

Key Verse: Luke 9:58 "*... Foxes have holes and the birds of the air have nests, but the Son of Man has nowhere to lay his head.*"

Read the last part of this chapter, and you get the distinct impression that Jesus didn't have the foggiest idea, when it came to public relations. Before you get defensive (as if Jesus needs defenders!), think about it for a moment.

Suppose you had the greatest message the world has ever heard, but it wasn't going all that well with the ratings. People were ignoring you at best, and persecuting you at worst. You've just had a bad day in Samaria when, along comes a bright-eyed idealist who just loves you and wants to follow you "wherever you go" (v.57). So what do you do? You sign him up! You give him your "now that I believe" follow-up manual, get his full name and address, put him on your mailing list, and make sure the nurture-group leader in his area gets him to the next house meeting. You pray with him and tell him he's made a wise decision.

What you don't do is highlight your personal poverty and imply in no uncertain terms that if he follows you he'll be a pauper, too. Nor do you turn to other would-be followers and tell them that it's either you or their bereaved families — "You go to that funeral and you can forget following me. You say goodbye to your family, and I say goodbye to you." Was Jesus insensitive here or what?

It appears He was. But then appearances can be misleading. There is another cliché, "what you see isn't always what you get". It could very well be that at this point in Jesus' ministry He was, in His eyes, becoming too "popular". More and more wanted to follow Him, but they were doing so for the wrong reasons. Jesus had to do some sifting of wheat from chaff. And I suspect Jesus' words to these idealists were meant not just for them but for the scores of would-be disciples who were within ear-shot.

Jesus wanted it to be known that there was a cost in following Him. He demanded singleness of purpose and maturity. He wanted people with an eye to the heavenly kingdom, feet on the ground, and back bent in doing good.

Grace isn't cheap!

Prayer for Today: *Lord Jesus, according to the grace given unto us, we determine to follow You as Your true disciples, whatever the cost may be.*

Read Luke 10   *May 7*

Key Verse: Luke 10:20 *"...do not rejoice...that the spirits are subject to you, but rather rejoice because your names are written in heaven."*

In the last chapter, we read of Jesus sending out the twelve disciples "to preach the kingdom of God and to heal the sick" (9:2). In this chapter, He sends out seventy more. It's in this context that Jesus says the famous words, "the harvest is plentiful, but the workers are few. Ask the Lord of the harvest, therefore, to send out workers into His harvest field" (v.2).

So the seventy rookies went out, and came back, a few days later, with a glowing report. "Lord, even the demons submit to us in Your name," they exulted. "We have power! Authority! We're special!" Or so they thought.

And they were. No doubt Jesus was pleased to hear it had gone so well. He had hand-picked these special people. They had gone out to preach, heal, and deliver — and they had succeeded. They tried to follow Jesus' example — and they did, with one glaring exception: they had become overly impressed with their spiritual power, especially as it related to their ability to rout demonic spirits. Spiritual pride was beginning to raise its ugly head.

Jesus put things in perspective. "It's no big deal about the demons," He said, in effect. "That's no reason to rejoice. Rather, rejoice that your names are recorded in heaven." As great as a miracle of deliverance or healing may be, it's small bananas compared to the greatest miracle of all — passing from death into life. Salvation is miracle number one; beside it the other miracles pale in significance.

God isn't impressed with a panoply of miracles and a plethora of miracle workers. Unlike humans, He's not moved by the outward show of things (after all, there are false miracles and false prophets who, on the outside, are very impressive). He *is* impressed with those He calls His children. He likes dependents, not co-deities.

Prayer for Today: *Lord Jesus, thank You for the assurance of our names written in heaven. We rejoice because of that day when You led us to receive by faith Your gift of eternal life according to Your promises.*

Read Luke 11   *May 8*

Key Verse: Luke 11:9 *"And I say to you, ask, and it will be given to you; seek, and you will find; knock, and it will be opened to you."*

Have you ever thought of prayer as a process? Usually we think of it only in terms of verbalizing: articulating a need. But if you look carefully at Jesus' teaching on prayer in this chapter, you begin to see prayer as far more than just talking to God.

As Jesus presents it, prayer is using your mouth, your head and your hands. You ask. You seek. You knock. Let's look at it.

We usually don't ask for something we already have, so when we ask for something, we're defining a need. Or, to put it another way, we're defining a goal. Seeking means actively looking here, there, and everywhere, in order to find something. That is, we're pursuing the options. And to do that we need to make some sort of plan. Knocking, on the other hand, is something you do when the options have been narrowed to a few key doors. There is a note of expectancy as you knock — an opportunity lies on the other side. So we knock. We work the plan.

Define the goal, make a plan, work the plan. Sounds like something from a business seminar. But the point is this: prayer is essentially active. It's not passive at all. Perhaps this is why our prayers are sometimes not answered — they're not finished. We're to ask, seek, and knock (all active verbs). After that, we're to receive, find, and enter. Don't sit back when you pray — go for it!

Prayer for Today: *Dear Lord, we're asking, seeking and knocking. Help us to be more persistent as was the person in our reading who needed bread. Grant that Your will shall be done on earth as it is in Heaven.*

Read Luke 12 *May 9*

Key Verse: Luke 12:1b *"Beware of the leaven of the Pharisees, which is hypocrisy."*

Nobody likes a hypocrite. There's something instinctive about this distaste — rather like our dislike for foul odors, snakes, and dishonest salesmen. We prefer people to be who they say they are. Regardless of the masks we ourselves may wear, we want the other guy to be transparent. We like an honest face. Indeed, one of the highest compliments we can pay a person is to recite the old adage of him, "what you see is what you get."

It's no secret Jesus gave the Pharisees a hard time; just like He would do to you and me. The Pharisees weren't any more enamoured of hypocrites than we are. And they'd be the last to admit any personal hypocrisy. Like us, they were concerned about God's word, about pleasing Him, attending weekly (in some cases, daily) services of worship and raising their children in the faith — in most areas of their lives they were just like present day North American conservative evangelical Christians — Orthodox in faith, moderate in practise. They were good guys.

That's why it stung when Jesus accused them of being inwardly filthy when they were so outwardly pure (11:39); or of neglecting justice and the love of God (11:42); or of being spiritually proud and self-serving (11:43).

But there was one accusation Jesus made which speaks volumes to me: "You load people down with burdens they can hardly carry" (11:46 NIV). This hits me because I'm a preacher, as well as a broadcaster and author. I have often moralized in my preaching, punctuating my sermons with idealisms, shoulds, coulds and black/white value judgments. I have laid guilt on people, crushing them with the burden of my view of righteousness. Little wonder there's been a significant fall-out rate over the years: being a human has a way of winning over being an angel.

It's taken me a few years, but now I try to point people to Jesus rather than standards. Not that standards are all bad, but when Jesus is magnified and glorified, moral standards seem to follow naturally.

I suppose it boils down to religion versus relationship.

Prayer for Today: *Lord Jesus, in our reading today You promised that if I would confess You, You would confess me before the angels. Enable me to so live that my lifestyle as well as my words will be a pure confession of You.*

Read Luke 13 & 14   *May 10*

Key Verse: Luke 14:33 *"...whoever of you does not forsake all he has cannot be My disciple."*

I don't like those words in the key verse. Nor do I like these words: "If anyone comes to Me and does not hate his father and mother, his wife and children, his brothers and sisters — yes, even his own life — he cannot be My disciple. And anyone who does not carry his cross and follow Me cannot be My disciple" (vss. 26,27 NIV). I dislike them, not just because they offend my values, but also because they seem out of character with Jesus, if taken at face value.

I say "out of character" for a number of reasons. First of all, Jesus had a high view of scripture, which included a high view of the ten commandments — one of which says, "Honour your father and mother..." Secondly, He had a high view of children — "suffer the little children to come unto Me..." Jesus respected the word of His Father which commands us to "train up a child in the way he should go..." — so how do you do this if you have deserted the child?

Obviously, Jesus was doing here what He often did as was the custom of a good semitic teacher: He used exaggeration for the sake of emphasis. He shocked people into seeing the point. The point here was simply that Jesus expects His disciples to put God and His kingdom first ("seek first the kingdom of heaven, and its righteousness..."), and personal concerns second ("...and all these things will be added unto you" — Matt.6:33).

He's a lover of our souls, but He's a jealous lover. Don't cross Him.

Prayer for today: O Father God, Your Son gave us goals which can only be accomplished by Your Spirit living in and through us. We're totally dependent on You!

Read Luke 15 & 16 *May 11*

Key Verse: Luke 16:31 *"If they do not hear Moses and the prophets, "...If neither will they be persuaded though one rise from the dead."*

It's amazing but true: there still are "Christians" who have a distinct prejudice against (if not an out-and-out hatred for) Jews. Three or four times a year, I receive mail from these anti-Semites. Usually their letters are more like tomes — overstuffed manila envelopes with articles, essays, facts and figures, all designed and tailored to make me believe there is a Jewish conspiracy to take over the world. It is hateful and disgusting. What's more, it's sinful.

Jesus was a Jew, and I love Him; I also love His people. That's one reason why my family and I gave seven years of our lives to living and working in Israel. I also have the highest respect for the disciples and the apostle Paul (all Jews) — so much so, that I follow their teaching and base my life on their interpretation of the words of Jesus. On top of that (or should I say, "foundational to that"), is my high view of Moses and the prophets. The "Old" Testament, as we call it, is the very root system of my Christian faith. Take the Old Testament away from me and you've uprooted me — focus only on the New Testament and you may appear alive for awhile, just like your Christmas tree appears to be living for a week or so in your house at Christmastime, but eventually my branches will turn brown.

In Luke 16, Jesus tells the story of the rich man and Lazarus. He quotes Abraham as saying that if "Moses and the prophets" can't convince a person of the reality of Heaven and Hell, then the resurrection won't do it either. Jesus' life and ministry was a fulfillment of the Old Testament. You can try to take Jesus out of the Old Testament — but you cannot take the Old Testament out of Jesus. Like love and marriage, they are inseparable. But don't call it a "mixed" marriage. Sure, the Old Testament is Jewish, but so is the New!

Prayer for Today: Dear Lord in our reading in Luke 15 You spoke again and again of finding that which was lost. Help us to help You look for the lost, bringing a precious person to You today.

Read Luke 17 & 18   *May 12*

Key Verse: Luke 18:13 *"...God be merciful to me a sinner!"*

The Bible doesn't always make an editorial comment about Jesus' parables, but Luke does so in this instance. The famous parable of the Pharisee and the tax collector is told to "some who were confident of their own righteousness and looked down on everybody else" (18:9 NIV). Of course, the temptation to us as we read, is to look down on the Pharisee. Human nature, as irrepressible as it is, will always manage to condescend somehow.

This parable is a classic. On one side you have a self-satisfied religious type. On the other side is a self-disgusted con artist. One enters confidently, arrogantly, even, into the temple — it is familiar and much loved territory. The other enters fearfully, regretfully, and awkwardly — the temple is foreign territory. The one saunters, the other grovels. And to the surprise of the listener, Jesus says God responds to the man with the dirty face, and rejects Mr. Clean. This doesn't seem fair, does it?

To appreciate the shock value of this parable, think of it in these terms: the Pharisee is you and the tax collector is a convicted rapist. You've never knowingly hurt anybody in your life. You've attended church faithfully, paid your tithes, and helped the poor. You are always ready to testify to your faith and intend to obey God and serve Him all your life. And, in all honesty, as you see it, God owes you something, for you've kept *your* part of the bargain.

On the other hand, the rapist has been nothing but trouble all his life. He was kicked around at home, so he lashed out at school. Abused by society, he paid it back with ever-increasingly abusive behavior. Finally, he went on a rampage, beating, stealing and raping. Now, as he enters the prison chapel, he throws himself on the floor in anguish, while you, on your monthly prison visitation, take a moment for prayer before the chapel service.

And guess what? God ignores you and honours him! He disregards your self-satisfied conversation and embraces his self-condemnation. What gives?

Simply this. That man recognizes his spiritual poverty and you don't. He cries for mercy, even as you casually converse. His feet are slipping into the pit; yours are merely slippered. He is in anguish; you are content.

Never forget Jesus' words in the Sermon on the Mount, "Blessed are the poor in spirit, for theirs is the kingdom of heaven"

(Mt. 5:3). Regardless of how wholeheartedly we've embraced Christ, it is only because He's embraced us first that we have any right to stand in His presence. And when He first embraced us, we were detestably filthy; as filthy as a rapist.

Prayer for Today: *"God, be merciful to me, a sinner". Grant, O Lord, that we may see ourselves as Paul saw himself, "Chiefest of sinners", and grant that we may live in a repentant attitude.*

Read Luke 19   May 13

Key Verse: Luke 19:44 *"... you did not know the time of your visitation."*

If you have read even a bit of the Bible, you're sure to have noticed the awfully serious view it takes of decision-making: especially those decisions about our relationship with God. When we're vague, or try to postpone, if not water down, the demands of the relationship, He is clear-cut and downright inflexible. We want qualifiers, maybe's, and wait-and-see's. He wants either/or. He will work for a while at winning us, but warns that His Spirit will not always wrestle with us. If we put the decision off He'll eventually stop trying to convince us, and the results, He warns, will be disastrous.

A case in point is Jesus weeping over Jerusalem. The city personifies the nation of Israel, Jesus' own and God the Father's chosen people. Notice that, even in the context of a heart-rending compassion, Jesus is gratingly blunt in His pronouncement of doom: "The days will come upon you when your enemies will build an embankment against you and encircle you and hem you in on every side. They will dash you to the ground, you and the children within your walls. They will not leave one stone on another..." (vss. 43,44). This is pretty hard stuff; it almost seems that Jesus is forseeing genocide here.

What makes it even more difficult is the seemingly schizophrenic nature of God in this passage. On the one hand, He loves His people with an everlasting love, on the other He pronounces judgment and appears to be prepared to sit back and let it happen. And this is all because His chosen ones "did not recognize the time of God's coming" to them.

The lesson? God is love and God is just, and won't extend His love forever, any more than He will postpone His judgment forever. It's scary, but true — when God speaks, we'd better listen.

Prayer for Today: *Lord God, please help us to listen and obey. We pledge our determination and You have pledged us Your grace. By grace through faith You save us. Thank You (Ephesians 2:8).*

Read Luke 20 & 21 *May 14*

Key Verse: Luke 21:4 *"all these people gave their gifts out of their wealth; but she out of her poverty..."*

The question occurring to me as I read this story is, "what would Jesus think or say about some modern ministries that unscrupulously bilk widows of their life savings?" We have no record of what Jesus said or did about this poor widow who put all she had to live on in the temple treasury. All we read is that Jesus saw her do it and was impressed.

What do you suppose motivated her? It was probably the first time she had done this; and probably the last. How often can you give all you have to live on before the well is completely dry, and you die? Maybe she had a great need and felt that her meagre gift was a part of expressing her deepest sincerity in petitioning God for help. Maybe she felt especially guilty about some secret sin. Or perhaps she was in such desperate straits that giving all she had was an act of frustration, anger, and acquiescence — a kind of financial suicide. Maybe she thought this might force God to intervene. Then again, maybe she gave out of total gratitude for some special answer to prayer. Who knows? But the point Jesus made was that she gave out of her poverty: her gift was costly.

Contrast this to the carefully measured gifts of the wealthy. Many of them, no doubt, were meticulous in their commitment to tithing — every month the first donation was a tithe to the temple. They perhaps even preached the importance of giving first to God before any other bill was paid, and I doubt the Lord would fault them for this. In fact, Jesus said nothing overtly negative about their donations. What He did say, however, related to the relative value of the gifts — not as men saw it, but as God saw it.

The gift of the wealthy was simply that — a gift. The gift of the widow was something else — it was a sacrifice — and sacrificial giving then, as now, was pretty much out of style.

Prayer for Today: *Our Heavenly Father, according to our Bible reading, this age will come to an end. Please give us the Spirit of giving to You now, because only what is given will last forever.*

Read Luke 22 *May 15*

Key Verse: Luke 22:29 *"I bestow upon you a kingdom, just as My Father bestowed one upon Me."*

Here's a passage of scripture that has been remarkably silent over the years. At least in sermons, that is. We have probably heard a few sermons on Jesus sending out the disciples without "purse, bag or sandals" — the point of our dependency on God was well made in all of them. In fact, the party line has been that if God calls you and sends you out, you can rely totally on Him and have no need of money, extra clothing, or a second pair of Adidas. And the stock response from the faithful, as this principle is preached, is, "Amen!"

But wait a minute! After the disciples affirm that they had no need the first time they were out there ministering without material resources, Jesus now tells them the rules have changed. "But now", He says, "if you have a purse, take it, and also a bag; and if you don't have a sword, sell your cloak and buy one." (v.36 NIV). Jesus is telling His disciples to buy a sword, and to sell their overcoat to get one? You mean defending yourself against an attack is more important in Jesus' eyes than defending yourself against the elements, and you need money and a suitcase as well? Where did you say that reference was again?

What's going on here? The real world, that's what. Jesus had already taught His disciples the lesson of complete submission to His will and total dependence upon His provision. Now, He was stressing the complementary role we can play in our ministries by good planning and responsible management. What's more, He was showing us that, as far as our physical safety is concerned, there are some "executive responsibilities" we have in assisting our heavenly Father and His ministering angels in this business of staying alive. Jesus wants us to be childlike — not childish.

Prayer for Today: *Father, as we learn both dependency on Your provision and our personal responsibilities, enable us to faithfully pray as Jesus taught us in this chapter, "Nevertheless, not my will but Yours be done."*

Read Luke 23

Key Verse: Luke 23:12 *"That very day Pilate and Herod became friends..."*

In this chapter and the latter half of the previous chapter, we read of the crucifixion. Some have called this the "Passion" narrative. In 22:47-53 we see Jesus arrested (even while His disciples were eager to use those newly purchased swords — "Lord, should we strike with our swords?" v.49b). Then, in vss. 54-62, we read of Peter's denial that he was a follower of Jesus. After this, Jesus is taken before Pilate and Herod, and then led to Golgotha. He dies and is buried. The story is over; or so His enemies thought.

What happened next must wait for Luke's concluding chapter. But there is something in this chapter which is very rarely commented on. It's a reference to two old enemies becoming friends.

We don't really have any information on why Herod and Pilate were enemies. Maybe it was due to a clash of authority. Both men were accountable to Rome, but Herod, as Tetrarch, had a bit more autonomy than Pilate, as the Governor. Perhaps Herod resented that his autonomy could be challenged or ignored by Pilate from time to time: he could "go over Herod's head" at will. And Pilate might have shared a common disgust for the paranoid Herod and flaunted it. But this is speculation.

For whatever reason, they were enemies, and Jesus made them friends. Isn't that ironic? Their new view of one another sprang, not from being new men, but from trying to deal with "that Man". They were both fascinated with and flummoxed by Jesus. Herod grew tired of his game with Jesus and had Him ridiculed and mocked. Pilate had Him crucified. Neither knew exactly why. "And it wasn't all bad — after all, it pleased the people and we've become friends!"

Jesus became a friend too: with sinners.

Prayer for Today: *Thank you Jesus that You're a friend of sinners. We need Your friendship. You've shown us the greatest love of all. You laid down Your life for Your friends (John 15:13).*

Read Luke 24 *May 17*

Key Verse: Luke 24:27 *"And beginning at Moses and all the Prophets, He expounded to them in all the Scriptures the things concerning Himself."*

The crucifixion was a real blow to Jesus' disciples. Not just the inner group of twelve, but all of Jesus' followers were devastated by the news of His death. It was a grim moment.

On Resurrection Day, two of Jesus' followers left Jerusalem to walk to Emmaus. They had heard the rumours of the empty tomb but were confused, rather than convinced. Depressed and disappointed, they were glumly walking along, discussing the events of the previous few days, when they were joined by a third man. He asked what they had been talking about. One of them, named Cleopas, responded rather curtly, "Are you the only one living in Jerusalem who doesn't know the things that have happened there in these days?"

Jesus feigned ignorance, "What things?", He asked. They went on to tell Him what He so intimately knew. After they had finished, He went on to explain that the Christ ("Messiah") had to undergo all these things in order to fulfil the writings of Moses and the Prophets, then He acted as if He was going farther than Emmaus. The disciples implored Him to stay the night. Over dinner it suddenly became clear. As He broke the bread and gave it to them, "their eyes were opened". But even as they gasped a greeting, He disappeared from their sight.

What a surprise! Especially to these thoroughly disappointed disciples. They had "hoped that He was the one who was going to redeem Isreael" (NIV), and He had died, just like any other zealot. Three years of hope and self-sacrifice had been dashed, and then this! An empty tomb, a flesh-and-blood appearance and disappearance! What was going on?

Here's what. Jesus *was* going to redeem Israel, not merely from Roman oppression, but from Satanic oppression. He was going to save His people from their sins. The eternal kingdom was at the door!

Prayer for Today: *Lord Jesus, reveal Yourself to us today as we walk the road of life. Help us the next days as we read Moses and the prophets for ourselves so we will know more of You.*

Introduction to
The Book of Numbers

The book of Numbers receives its name from the two numberings of the Israelites which are contained in the book. The first census was shortly after their departure from Egypt, while in the desert of Sinai (chapter 1). The second was of the new generation about thirty-nine years later, while on the plains of Moab before proceeding to the Promised Land (chapter 26). The Hebrew title for this book is taken from the first word of the Hebrew text, *Wayyedabber*, meaning "And He Said", but it is more commonly referred to as *Bemidbar*, "In the Wilderness", from the fifth Hebrew word of the first sentence, and this title better describes the content of the book.

This fourth book of Moses continues the redemptive story of the nation of Israel. It starts where the second book, Exodus, ended. We read of the nation's organization, travels and wanderings, and sadly, also learn of their disobedience and rebellion which turned a short journey to Canaan into forty years of wandering in the wilderness. Yet God was faithful and lovingly sustained His people. God is also just, righteous and holy, and because of their continued disobedience, we read of many occasions of His wrath upon them which led to severe punishment and chastening. The book serves as a warning against unbelief and illustrates well the spiritual warfare of believers.

The theme of Numbers seems to be the love and justice of God which are always combined in perfect harmony. The Apostle Paul wrote concerning the "goodness and severity" of God (Romans 11:22), and this aptly describes the main topic of the book.

Numbers covers a period of thirty-nine years, however most of the years are unrecorded. We learn of the main events, fascinating stories, the preparation, service, warfare, and walk of God's redeemed people before they entered the Promised Land. The organization of the Levites as a people separated unto God is seen in this book, and throughout it God's holiness is evident. Also evident are His all-sufficiency and omnipotence which are seen through the many miraculous events that take place.

Read Numbers 1 *May 18*

Key Verse: Numbers 1:45 *"So all who were numbered of the children of Israel... were able to go to war in Israel."*

One month after the Tabernacle had been erected (Exodus 40:17), Moses took a census of all the men of Israel 20 years old and upward who were eligible to bear arms and go to battle. It marked the start of preparation for the Israelites to move onward which was to begin in just 19 days (Numbers 10:11-12). They had to be well-organized and ready for war, since on their way to Canaan they would encounter many enemies. Only true Israelites, not those of the "mixed multitude", were to enlist. Through the census, they knew who were the strangers among the people of God, and those not in covenant relationship with Him could not engage in His battles. The Church of Jesus Christ is often pictured as an army engaged in a battle with the enemy, Satan. All who are in the New Covenant relationship with Christ must enlist as soldiers for His cause and "wage the good warfare" (1 Timothy 1:18; 2 Timothy 2:3-4).

The words, "the Lord spoke to Moses" (1:1), are found about eighty times in the Book of Numbers. This is a clear indication that Moses was indeed the author. God directed His steps, and the census was a direct command from Him. God also appointed an able man from each tribe to help Moses and Aaron calculate the numbers. What a great responsibility these twelve men were given, and how honoured they were to have their names specifically mentioned by God and to be chosen to serve Him in this way! Those who are capable and willing to fulfil the task will be chosen and honoured by God.

The tribe of Judah was the largest, and therefore they were the leaders in the march (1:26-27). The total number of the census came to 603,550 fighting men. Some liberal commentators have expressed doubt that the actual number was so high, because it would mean that there would have been over two million people in the wilderness. However, this type of thinking minimizes God's ability to care for them all, as this book illustrates He did. Exodus 1:7 describes their remarkable growth while in Egypt, so much so that the Egyptians felt they were a threat to their national security (Exodus 1:9-10). The census served to prove God's faithfulness in keeping His promise to Abraham, and it is clear evidence of His blessings upon them (Gen. 12:2). It also is evidence of the great care God took of His people. He is called the Shepherd of Israel (Psalm 80:1): each shepherd takes count of his sheep and knows each one, for each is valuable and he does not want one to be lost. Jesus is the Good Shepherd of those who follow Him today. He knows those who are His own and calls them by name (John 10:3,11,14).

The census excluded the tribe of Levi which was exempted from military service because God had called them to serve in the Tabernacle (1:49-50). Ministers of the Lord should not become entangled with things that would distract them from their holy calling. The tribe of Levi was honoured over the others because they had shown themselves faithful in the incident of the golden calf (Exodus 32:26). Only they could touch or see the holy things of God; no one else was permitted to even come close, lest the judgment of death come upon him. The Levites were to camp around the Tabernacle in order to protect the sanctity of it and prevent the wrath of God upon those who might sin and defile it (1:51-53).

No one is worthy to have fellowship with God and behold His holiness and glory until they have been called by His grace into fellowship with His Son Jesus Christ — only then are they made worthy. Isaiah prophesied that God would show His glory to the Gentiles, and He will "take some of them for priests and Levites" (Isaiah 66:21).

Prayer for today: *Thank You, Father, that in the New Agreement between You and Your only begotten Son, everybody is welcome to come boldly unto the Throne of Grace to find help in time of need.*

Read Numbers 2 *May 19*

Key Verse: Numbers 2:2 *"Everyone of the children of Israel shall camp by his own standard...some distance from the tabernacle of meeting."*

The census not only numbered the fighting men, but organized each person into his proper tribe (Numbers 1). With this accomplished, the Lord told Moses the military plan of having four squadrons, made up of three tribes, that were to have specific places when encamped or on the march. When encamped, the Tabernacle was to be central, with the priests and Levites surrounding it. Out of reverence, each tribe was assigned a specific place at a distance surrounding it, that all would have their eyes upon it. Not only was the Tabernacle to be central in position, it was to be central in their lives and the focal point of their whole society.

No invader could come close to the Tabernacle without meeting much resistance from the soldiers. It was to be well-protected and honoured, for it represented the presence of God in their midst. We, also, must stand strong to defend the Lord's honour and protect

His sacred institutions. However, unlike the Israelite tribes which were ordered to remain at a distance, we are welcome to draw near to the throne of God. May our Lord, by His grace, keep us ever so close to Him, that our eyes will always be upon Him.

The tribe of Judah, being the largest and strongest, was given the most honoured place (prophecy fulfilled, Genesis 49:8). Their encampment was toward the rising sun to the east of the Tabernacle, facing its gate and the encampment of the priestly family. They also led in the march. However, the greatest honour given to this tribe was that through it the royal line and the Messiah would come (Genesis 49:10). The leader of the tribe, Nahshon, is listed among the ancestors of Jesus (Matthew 1:4).

God Himself appointed the place each tribe was to occupy. If Moses had made the choices, there could have been envy, quarrelling, and charges that he was partial, but we read how "the children of Israel did according to all that the Lord commanded Moses" (2:34). Likewise, the people of God today are to be obedient to God and content in the place He has put them, and they are to keep in good order and unity; this glorifies God and leads to the building up of His Kingdom.

Each Israelite knew exactly where he belonged in the camp. They could not set up their tent wherever they pleased, but only where God had placed them, for our God is a "God of order, not confusion". The divine order of the whole camp site and the grand military precision of their march must have displayed great unity and beauty (Numbers 24:5). They were to camp, as well as march, beside their tribe's standard or banner. These served to distinguish between the tribes and to gather and keep them together. Under their own banner they would find safety. The prophet Isaiah wrote concerning the Messiah, Jesus, that He would stand as a banner that the Gentiles would seek, a place of glorious rest (Isaiah 11:10). Those that serve the Lord Jesus and gather unto Him find safety there and can say with joyous hearts, "His banner over me is love" (Song of Solomon 2:4).

Prayer for Today: *Lord, please show us our place in Your plan for Your church and help us to keep our lives in order within the whole body of the people of God. May we move in unity with all our brothers and sisters in Christ.*

Read Numbers 3 *May 20*

Key Verse: Numbers 3:12 *"I Myself have taken the Levites from among the children of Israel instead of every first born... the Levites shall be Mine."*

In this chapter, we see the separation of a single tribe, the Levites, for divine service and their organization by God, expressing the importance of worship. Their census, however, was different from that of the other tribes. They were not to be counted for military duty, but all the males one month old and upward were counted (3:15), for they were being set apart for the sacred service of the Lord.

We learn that God appointed Aaron to be chief over the Levites and they were to aid the priests who had a great job to do. To those who are called by God for a large task, He will give the help they need. The Levites were responsible firstly to God, then to Aaron and the priests; and the Levities were responsible to serve all the congregation of Israel. They were entrusted with the people's spiritual well-being and enabled to have access to God.

Aaron's two younger sons were wise (unlike their two older brothers, Nadab and Abihu; Leviticus 10) for they remained under the close watch of their father (3:4), making sure that all was done just as the Lord had prescribed. They took heed to the warnings of God and proved themselves worthy. The elder of the two, Eleazar, was chief over the leaders of the Levites (3:32), and later replaced his father Aaron as high priest. Ithamar was appointed by God to be in charge of the Tabernacle (4:28,33).

The descendants of Levi were taken by God in place of the first-born Israelites whom God had made provision to save in Egypt with the Passover (Exodus 12:12-13; 13:1). Because of the sin of the people, God limited His choice to the tribe of Levi, who had shown their loyalty to Him by going on His side with Moses in the sinful incident of the golden calf (Exodus 32:26). It was also out of the graciousness of God that He took the Levites, rather than having the families of every tribe part with their beloved first-born son. In this way, all the families could remain as a unit working together. Yet for us, God, in His great love, did not spare His own beloved first-born son but gave Him for us (Romans 8:32).

When it was discovered that there were 273 more first-born males among the tribes than there were Levites to replace them, those extra men were to be redeemed from service by the payment of a certain measure of weight in silver. The church of Jesus Christ is called the Church of the First-Born (Colossians 1:15-18), and we who are members of His church have not been redeemed with silver, as those of the Old Covenant were, but by the precious blood of the Son of God, our Lord Jesus Christ who has made us kings and priests to God (1 Peter 1:18-19; Revelation 1:5-6).

The descendants of Levi's three sons were assigned specific duties. The Gershonites were responsible for the tent and coverings; the Kohathites (the family of Moses and Aaron) for the inner, most sacred furniture; the Merarites for the external parts of the Tabernacle. It must have been marvelous to see these well-trained teams put up and take down this large structure. Their three-fold duties were basically to serve, help and guard. They encamped on the three sides of the Tabernacle with Moses and the priestly family of Aaron in the honoured place at the east side. Upon the threat of death, no "outsider", that is anyone lacking the authorization, was to come near when the priests and Levites were attending to their sacred duties (3:10); for services to the Lord may be performed only by those whom the Lord appoints.

Prayer for today: *Lord, while Israel fought against flesh-and-blood enemies, we don't. Your Word says our fight is against principalities and powers and the rulers of the darkness of this world. We need Your supernatural intervention for victory in our lives, even as You intervened again and again for Israel. Thank You!*

Read Numbers 4 *May 21*

Key Verse: Numbers 4: 47,49 *"From thirty . . . to fifty years old, everyone who came to do the work of service and the work of bearing burdens in the tabernacle . . . were numbered by the hand of Moses . . . as the Lord commanded . . ."*

Here again we find more details concerning the organization and the specific ministries of the Levites. We learn of a second census to establish the number of Levites from each family that were eligible and able to serve in the tasks of the tabernacle. Their main responsibilities were to guard the Tabernacle, transport it, assemble and disassemble it; all with great care and reverence. These divinely given directions emphasize the holiness of the sacred symbols of worship which were to be carefully guarded and respected; not to be treated in a casual way, nor made to be something common.

The Kohathites, the family of Moses and Aaron, had the important ministry of carrying the most holy articles of the Tabernacle. Before they could do their job, Aaron and his sons were to wrap and cover the pieces of furniture and the different articles in the prescribed manner. The priests were also to insert the poles that the Kohathites would use to carry them upon their shoulders. Upon the threat of death, they were not to touch, nor even take a glance at the holy things. The responsibility was put upon the priests to warn the

Kohathites of the danger involved in their duties, for they were especially exposed to the risk of violating the law since they worked so closely with these items as assistants to the priests (4:15, 18; cf. 2 Samuel 6:6-7). Eleazer, the son of Aaron and the future high priest, was to personally carry the holy oil and incense, as well as supervise and oversee all the activities of the Kohathites that they might not violate the law nor handle their loads carelessly, but remain safe from God's wrath.

The Kohathites did their jobs in fear, but for us today, through Jesus Christ, there is a lovely change. Those who minister before God need not fear getting too close to His holiness, because we have been privileged: "we have seen with our eyes, which we have looked upon, and our hands have handled, concerning the Word of life" (1 John 1:1). Jesus Christ was made manifest to us, and His blood "cleanses us from all sin" (1 John 1:7). With this knowledge, our "joy may be full" (1 John 1:4) and we may "come boldly to the throne of grace" (Hebrews 4:16).

We may find it hard to see the jobs of the Gershonites (in charge of carrying the tent and the curtains), and Merarites (responsible for the smaller things like the tent pegs) as sacred duties, but they were, for it was God's calling for their lives. In fact, all the Levites were called in the service of hard work, and each was to do this kind of work for a period of 20 years, from ages 30 to 50 (4:39). It was not the most glamourous or exciting work, but was necessary that the work of the Lord might go smoothly and with unity. Those who do more menial jobs should still do them as a ministry unto the Lord, for that is where the Lord has placed them. We need to submit to the Lordship of Jesus Christ and strive to glorify Him in all things, for that which is done as unto the Lord, no matter how small, will not go unrewarded.

Prayer for today: *Father God, please reveal to each of us our calling. Grant us grace to be willing to do the most humble tasks in Your service.*

Read Numbers 5   *May 22*

Key Verse: Numbers 5:28 *"But if the woman has not defiled herself, and is clean, then she shall be free and may conceive children."*

In this chapter, we see that some of the regulations of purity that were given in the book of Leviticus are now being put into effect. Lepers and others who were ceremonially unclean were to be put outside the camp to live apart from the rest of the congregation. This was to illustrate the importance of keeping sin and any kind of defilement away from the camp and their lives, for they were admonished over and over again to be holy, and their standard of holiness was God Himself (Leviticus 11:44).

This standard has not changed: We who follow God must also exhibit holiness in our lives. The church today would do well to follow the example of the early church in disciplining those of their fellowship who are in sin. God has provided for the church to judge and discipline such acts in a prescribed, loving manner (Matthew 18:15-17), for if they do not: "a little leaven leavens the whole lump" (1 Corinthians 5:6,11-12). Sin can be infectious, and therefore God's people must separate themselves from it. God's presence will not abide where there is defilement and sin.

A further provision of separation from sin was demanded by one who had transgressed and sinned against another person. In this case, a public confession of the sin and restitution was required. For transgressions which did not involve restitution to be made to another person, the payment of restitution was to go directly to the priest as an honourarium. God shared with His ministers those things which belonged to Him.

A large portion of this chapter served to show to God's people the importance of separation from the sin of marital infidelity. The sanctity of the marriage bed was, and still is, extremely important in the sight of God. If an Israelite man and woman were caught in adultery, the penalty was death for both (Leviticus 20:10). God provided an unusual test of guilt or innocence for the wife whose husband suspected her of committing adultery and yet did not have proof, in which God alone would be the judge, for He knows and sees all things. This test was established to help produce a high level of marital purity within the covenant community.

There was nothing in the water itself (5:17) which could bring about the curse for one who was guilty; only God could do this and since He established this test, He would preside over it and intervene with His judgment. It seems that the figurative language used in curse (5:21) means the woman would not be able to bear children, but the opposite would be true if she was found innocent: her fertility would be a blessing from God because she was found clean. Not only would she be blessed, but we also read, "she shall be free" (5:28). Sin brings bondage, but purity before God brings freedom.

This test would protect the unjustly charged woman and God would vindicate her. The innocent woman would find harmony within her home and reconciliation with her husband (healing of her marriage). Since his jealousy had proven to be unwarranted, the test would kill the root of jealousy so it would not grow and cause destruction (Song of Solomon 8:6). God desires to see harmony in our lives and between marriage partners, but purity and keeping His laws are essential for harmony.

Prayer for today: O Holy God, we pray for hearts filled with love, purity and understanding. Help us to be like Jesus in forgiving others and in calling for repentance. May the fear of You, O Lord, come on all of us as it did upon the early church.

Read Numbers 6 *May 23*

Key Verse: Numbers 6:24-26 *"The Lord bless you and keep you; The Lord make His face shine upon you, and be gracious to you; The Lord lift up His countenance upon you, and give you peace."*

The very important Nazarite vow of consecration is detailed in this chapter. The word "Nazarite" comes from the Hebrew verb "nazar", meaning "to dedicate" or "to separate". It was a voluntary expression of love and devotion to God by living a holy life which is separated to Him (6:8). Once this most serious vow was made, it became obligatory and binding. Both men and women could choose to become Nazarites for a certain period of time or for life (e.g. Samson and John the Baptist). Jesus was not a Nazarite; His life was already perfect, holy and sanctified. He was a "Nazarene", meaning someone who came from the city of Nazareth.

The Nazarites were not to drink or eat from any fruit of the vine which symbolized joy, rather their joy was to come from God alone. Also, they were not to cut their hair; this would distinguish them as being separated to God for a life of holiness. They were not to touch any dead body, causing them to become defiled, for death is the result of sin (Genesis 2:17). At the end of the period of separation, there were to be several offerings to the Lord which were very costly, but it seems they could be paid for by others (Acts 21:24); therefore, even the poor could find the means to fulfil that which was required. It also included the burning of his or her hair (6:18) which had grown during the specified time period. This was a further expression of a life totally committed to God and symbolized that the Nazarite had, in a sense, offered himself as "a living sacrifice, holy, acceptable to God" (Romans 12:1). The Apostle Paul must have understood the deep spiritual significance of this vow, for he himself took a Nazarite vow (Acts 18:18; 21:24).

Numbers 6 has one of Scripture's most beautiful and famous blessings. The Lord taught it to Moses who, in turn, was to teach Aaron and his sons, so that with it they might bless all the children of Israel. In all three sections of this lovely Hebrew poem, the Lord's name (Yahweh) is emphasized. The Israelites were to openly declare the Name of God, for it was to be put on them as a witness to the one and only Holy God; then God promised to bless them (6:27). Each of the three lines of this benediction promises two blessings: "The Lord bless you and keep you" (6:24) — they would receive all good things from God and be protected from any harm (kept safe in His loving arms); "The Lord make His face shine upon you, and be gracious to you" (6:25) — they would be happy and granted real life (Proverbs 16:15), be acceptable, favoured, and shown mercy; "The Lord lift up His countenance upon you and give you peace" (6:26) — God would give special attention and care for their good. The final blessing is that of "shalom", translated "peace'; this is a comprehensive term meaning: wholeness, health, contentment, security, friendship, total well-being and, most importantly, inner peace with God and spiritual blessings which can come only from Him (Ephesians 1:3).

To receive blessings from God, we first need to openly and unashamedly put His Name upon ourselves (6:27), and to separate ourselves from sin, like the Nazarite who became totally consecrated to Him. This may mean giving up certain fleeting pleasures of life (like the fruit of the vine for the Nazarite), but the joy of the Lord that results, and the joy everlasting, far outweigh any earthly pleasures.

Prayer for today: Lord, Jehovah, grant us Your grace to separate ourselves from any unclean thing, and not just from some things, but grant us to be separated to Your will and purpose. Thank You for Your blessings as we serve You.

Read Numbers 7   *May 24*

Key Verse: Numbers 7:4-5 *"Then the Lord spoke to Moses, saying, 'Accept these from them, that they may be used in doing the work of the tabernacle of meeting'."*

This chapter is the second longest in the whole Bible (Psalm 119 is the longest). It gives a detailed description of the many expensive free-will gifts and offerings which the leaders of the twelve tribes brought to the Lord. They all recognized the importance of worship to God. These were the same men whose leadership was reaffirmed by God in the first chapter of Numbers.

The gifts the leaders gave first were very necessary and practical: six carts and twelve oxen (7:3) for the purpose of transporting the Tabernacle. Moses gave these to the Gershonites and Merarites for moving their part of the Tabernacle. The Kohathites, however, were not given carts, for the Most Holy things were only to be carried on poles over their shoulders (7:7-9); the later disregard of this by King David and the Levites of his day resulted in a man's death (2 Samuel 6:3, 6-7).

On twelve successive days, each leader from the twelve tribes came to the Tabernacle on his assigned day and brought many identical gifts and offerings on the occasion of the dedication of the altar (7:11). The order in which the leaders were to come and present their gifts was the same as in the march (Numbers 2). We may wonder why there is so much repetition and be tempted to quickly skim over all these descriptions, but God did not. He saw to it, by the inspiration of His Holy Spirit, that all the names of the different leaders from each tribe and their separate and sacrificial gifts, however identical, were still individually mentioned in this record of history that we have preserved for our reading today. This expresses the special care and concern that God had for each of His tribes. Because they honoured Him with these generous gifts, He would do this honour for them (1 Samuel 2:30). Each time one of the Lord's people brings honour to Him, or gives sacrificially to His work, it is recorded in heaven, and that one will be honoured by the Lord.

The repetition also served to emphasize that since all the tribes donated equally to the service of the Tabernacle, they all had equal right to worship there. The equal gifts would also prevent any rivalry or pride of one tribe that may have been wealthier and able to give more. It also created a sense of unity in their purpose which would glorify God all the more. The spirit of generous giving the tribes displayed would serve as an example to their people, teaching them to do the same. It is interesting that this passage, listing all the gifts given to God, immediately follows the beautiful blessing of Numbers 6:24-26. Our response to the blessings of God should be to give Him gifts in love and thankfulness, as did the Israelites.

When all the offerings for the dedication of the altar had been received, Moses went into the house of God to converse with Him. Now the Lord spoke to Moses in an audible voice from above the mercy seat within His newly consecrated dwelling, not from the fiery mountain top. In Moses, the people had an advocate with God, but we have an ever better advocate, our Lord Jesus, through whom all who believe in Him can go before God and commune with Him.

Read Numbers 8 & 9 May 25

Key Verse: Numbers 8:11 *"Aaron shall offer the Levites before the Lord, as though a wave offering from the children of Israel, that they may perform the work of the Lord."*

The Levites had already been chosen, counted and organized; now we see their consecration for ministry in the Tabernacle. The ceremony was done in the sight of all the congregation of Israel, who put their hands on the heads of all the Levites, symbolizing their substitution for all the first-born (3:12-13). It was a solemn and sacred time, for the dedication of a life to the Lord is very serious and should be publically expressed, testifying that God has cleansed them from sin and has authority and Lordship over their life. Clearly, the wave offering of the Levites (8:11, 21) indicated that they were given over totally to God as a living sacrifice, that they might be acceptable to His service and do His will (Romans 12:1-2). The Lord then gave the Levites to the priests to help them in certain capacities of ministry, as well as serving as guards to protect the sacredness of the Tabernacle, thereby preventing any outbreak of God's wrath upon the Israelite community (8:19).

The ceremony was mainly one of purification as was evident in their shaving the hair off their bodies, washing their clothes and being sprinkled with water (8:7). The ceremony of consecration for the priests was different from that of the Levites, since the priests were especially consecrated to holiness for service within the sanctuary. As well as being washed with water, the priests had special garments that were anointed with holy oil and had the blood applied (Leviticus 8). The various sacrifices for the Levites were to atone for their sins, signifying inner cleansing. Those who work for the Lord today must first be made pure through the substitutionary atonement of Jesus Christ.

Before the Levites could enter active service, it is likely, as rabbinic tradition explains, that at age twenty-five they began a period of five years of preparation to be taught the things of the Lord and learn as apprentices (8:24). Then, at age thirty (4:3), the real service began. At fifty, they were required to leave the strenuous work, but could still be of assistance to the younger Levites, and surely they who were well-experienced, older and wiser, would serve as advisors and teachers, and continue to be guards for the Holy things.

Chapter nine expresses the graciousness of God. His gracious provision is evident in His reply to Moses concerning the men who had to miss the second Passover celebration (Exodus 12; Leviticus 23:4-5) because of being ceremonially unclean (9:6). Moses wisely told the men to wait while he went and sought the Lord. When we are in doubt about a spiritual matter, we too should seek the Lord and search His Word for guidance. God answered Moses with a merciful solution and yet He did not compromise; those who had missed the Passover celebration on the prescribed date could celebrate it one month later (9:10-12). Even the stranger or gentile among them who followed the ways of God might join in the Passover (9:14), but the Israelite who intentionally disobeyed and neglected it was to be "cut off" (excommunicated or killed).

The graciousness of God is also seen in the magnificent way He guided and protected His children with the pillar of cloud which hovered over the Tabernacle. This was no ordinary cloud, for it represented the presence of God among His covenant people. It had the brightness of fire by night, and God moved it when He desired to lead them to another camp site. We also would do well to always follow God's leading; not by a visible pillar of cloud, since "we walk by faith, not by sight" (2 Corinthians 5:7). This is the safest way to travel along life's paths. Following our own way leads to death (Proverbs 14:12), but Jesus said, "I am the way, the truth, and the life". Through faith in Him we find the only way to peace with God and everlasting life (John 14:6).

Prayer for today: *Lord, we seek You for guidance and claim Your promise that if we will acknowledge You in all our ways and lean not unto our own understanding, You will direct our paths.*

Read Numbers 10 & 11 *May 26*

Key Verse: Numbers 11:23 *"Has the Lord's arm been shortened? Now you shall see whether My word will befall you or not."*

Before the Israelites could begin their journey, God gave the final necessary details for their orderly march. Various distinguishing trumpet blasts served to summon the people, indicate certain feasts, give a warning, sound an alarm of war, unite the people and indicate times to advance. In obeying the sounds of the trumpet, they were obeying God, for Moses would order the blasts only after hearing from the Lord. One day there will come a heavenly trumpet sound signalling the meeting of the believers in the air with the Lord (1 Thessalonians 4:16).

After the Israelites were camped in the desert of Sinai for about a year, and after everything was put in order as the Lord commanded, He lifted the cloud from over the sanctuary and their journey to the Promised Land began. The twelve tribes, priests and Levites all took their proper places according to the instructions of the Lord. It was only by divine leading and the people's obedience that an orderly march of so vast a multitude was possible. We read that the Lord led them to a resting place (10:33), for the journey through that rough terrain was not easy, but with God's guidance it was made possible.

After only three days of the journey, the children of Israel began to complain. They took their eyes off God and looked at their situation in the bleak wilderness. God's anger was aroused and His judgment fell upon them by a fire until Moses interceded. Many of those who were farthest from God's sanctuary were consumed (11:1). They were probably the mixed multitude, most of whom had no desire to draw near to God and had stirred up discontentment, having a bad influence upon the Israelites, causing them to become dissatisfied with the manna God had given and to long for the foods they had eaten in Egypt. People who are not interested in spiritual things and always complain about their situation are not good company for one seeking to follow the Lord.

Moses was greatly disturbed and cried out to God, showing how very human he was and how great a burden it was for him to lead such a people. God did not want Moses to bear this burden alone, nor does He want us to be heavy-laden with burdens. He would gladly release stress from His people, if they would but ask and give it over to Him (Matthew 11:28). God was merciful to Moses and understood his discouragement. Likewise, He understands us when we are in the midst of trials. He will take us through them, lifting us up and giving us comfort.

God made Moses' load lighter by the appointment of the seventy men to be of assistance. Upon these He placed the same Spirit as He had given Moses. Moses, being humble and not seeking self-glory, was pleased with this, wishing that all the people had God's Spirit upon them (11:29). The work of the Holy Spirit is clearly evident throughout the whole Bible. Just as His Spirit was necessary upon the leaders then, so it is needful for spiritual leaders today.

God's second answer to Moses' dilemma concerning the people's lustful request for meat was to miraculously send the quail around their camp that they might be easily caught (11:31-32). However, it proved to show the foolishness of their desire, for they ended up being sick of it after one month of nothing but quail. Those who gluttonously gorged themselves, eating to satisfy their greedy, sinful lusts (without thanks to God for His provision), were struck by a fatal plague, killing many; so the meaning of the place is "graves of lust (craving)" (11:34).

The Lord proved to everyone that He was able to do what He had told Moses (11:23; cf. Isaiah 59:1-2). He did oblige them and gave them their request — a request which was not in His will. So the result was "leanness into their soul" (Psalm 106:15; cf. 78:26-31). Let us desire only those things which are pure and in keeping with the Lord's desires, that our souls may be nourished (Philippians 4:8; Colossians 3:2), for "godliness with contentment is great gain" (1 Timothy 6:6).

Prayer for today: *Lord, You said that if we would delight ourselves in You, You would give us the desires of our hearts, and because we do delight in You, we want only what You want. Please continue to reveal Your will to us in Your Word and by Your Spirit.*

Read Numbers 12 *May 27*

Key Verse: 12:3 *"Now the man Moses was very humble, more than all men who were on the face of the earth."*

The sad incident recorded in this chapter took place as the children of Israel were traveling northward to the Promised Land. Moses had come up against many difficulties during the journey (chapter 11), and this time it came not from the congregation, but from within his own family.

God had put Moses in a very special and unique place, more special than any other prophet (12:6-7; cf. Hebrews 3:3-6), yet he remained humble "more than all men" (12:3) and he did not seek self-glory, nor have the pretence of being humble (e.g.11:29). Jesus, the perfect example of leadership, was Himself meek and said "blessed are the meek" (Matthew 11:29; 5:5). Some might wonder how Moses could write this about himself. We believe all that he wrote was directed by the Holy Spirit, so he was like an objective and submissive servant, obeying all that God commanded Him to write. Moses even wrote of the more negative aspects of his own character, like his anger and sin (20:9-13). The fact that nothing is hidden attests to the Scripture's divine inspiration.

It seems Moses' older brother and sister, Aaron and Miriam, both known to be prophets and leaders among the people (Exodus 7:1; 15:20), were unlike their meek brother and desired more glory.

They were jealous of Moses and his high and respected position and used the occasion of his marriage to an Ethiopian/Cushite woman to begin whispering against him, but God hears all things. This wife would not have been Zipporah (Exodus 3:1; 4:24-26; she may have died), because the event referred to here seems to be recent. The marriage, however, was lawful, for Moses did not receive any rebuke from God, and surely she was a converted, godly woman who may have left with them from Egypt, or a Cushite from Arabia who dwelt in the Sinai region. Only the anointed priests were restricted to marrying an Israelite (Leviticus 21:14), and no one was to marry a Canaanite (Exodus 34:16). Miriam and Aaron complained out of jealousy and their desire to make Moses seem less in other people's eyes so they would seem better. God will only honour those who are humble and seek the good of others. The Bible teaches us to esteem others better than ourselves and to not speak against those in leadership (Phillipians 2:3; 1 Thessalonians 5:12-13).

Moses did not have to defend himself; God came to his defense. Because Miriam could not enter into the sanctuary, God, in the pillar of cloud, moved to the outer gate of the Tabernacle where He sternly confronted Miriam and Aaron with their sin. He vindicated Moses and reaffirmed the special place and high calling that only he had (12:6-8). How then could they do this evil, not only against Moses, but against the Lord as well, who had put Moses in that place of leadership? God's justice demanded punishment and since, as the Hebrew text indicates, it was Miriam who had instigated this rebellion (12:1), she was struck with leprosy. Aaron, as the high priest, could not become leprous and continue to perform the holy duties with which God had privileged him. Aaron immediately repented and called Moses his "Lord", showing him due respect. Moses was kind and forgiving, and with his intercessory plea, God in His mercy and forgiveness would heal Miriam, but first she was to be punished and made humble by remaining an outcast for seven days (cf. Leviticus 14:8).

This event served to illustrate that if a leader sinned, he or she was to be rebuked openly (1 Timothy 5:20). This would also cause more respect for the authority of the one whom God had appointed. Likewise, we need to show great respect for those whom God has appointed as leaders over His Church. Rather than complaining about a weakness they may have (for no one is perfect, except God), we need to lift them up, encourage them, and always emphasize their more positive aspects. When a person gossips against another, it not only causes harm to the one against whom it is directed, but also to the gossiper, the hearer, and the Lord, who feels deeply the hurts of others.

Prayer for today: *Lord God, we praise You for Your gift of leadership. We pray for our leaders in the Church and also in the Government. Cause us to be helpful to those who carry the burdens of leadership.*

Read Numbers 13 & 14 *May 28*

Key Verse: Numbers 13:30 *"Caleb...said, 'Let us go up at once and take possession, for we are well able to overcome it'."*

Moses had planned to go directly into Canaan from Sinai, but those plans were changed drastically. In Deuteronomy 1:19-24, Moses gave more background information about what had happened. We learn that it was the people's idea to first spy out the land before entering. Moses complied and the Lord allowed it, possibly as a test of faith, but they desperately failed.

The twelve able men, a leader from each tribe (except Levi), were chosen to go throughout the land and bring back a detailed report, as well as a sample of the fruit. This expedition was not really necessary, and it displayed a lack of faith, for God had already told them all they needed to know (Exodus 3:8; cf.Ezekiel 20:6). The people should have believed His promise that He would go before them and give them the land.

The mission was successfully accomplished and after forty days the spies returned. At first their report was in agreement concerning the land: "It truly flows with milk and honey" (13:27), meaning it was very fertile, and they brought proof, (13:23). However, concerning the inhabitants and their strength, it was ten against two. The ten, because of fear and lack of faith in God, said the people of the land were too strong for them and exaggerated the report saying, "we saw giants...and we were like grasshoppers" (13:33). These fearful men brought discouragement and instilled fear in the hearts of all the people who then complained bitterly, even to the point of wishing to return to Egypt! Had they forgotten so soon their sorrow in slavery (Exodus 2:23) and the miracles of God?

Only Caleb and Joshua trusted in God that it was possible to be victorious and possess the land. These remarkable men of faith and courage boldly stood up against the majority opinion. Truly, the majority is not always right, and the truth is not often popular. Believers today may find themselves standing alone for the Lord at work, home, or school, but do not be discouraged: "If God is for us, who can be against us?" (Romans 8:31). He "gives us the victory through our Lord Jesus Christ" (1 Corinthians 15:57), and although we can expect trials to come our way, Jesus said, "be of good cheer, I have overcome the world" (John 16:33).

Caleb's and Joshua's attempts to persuade the Israelites not to fear proved futile (14:8-9). The people became angry and even suggested they should choose another leader to take them back to Egypt (14:4). This was, in fact, a rejection of God, and if it had not been for His intervention in protecting Moses, Aaron, Joshua and Caleb, they would have been stoned (14:10).

The Lord's anger was justifiably stirred against Israel for their disobedience and faithlessness. As it was with their sin of the golden calf, God once again expressed His desire to destroy and disinherit the sinful Israelites and raise up a new chosen nation through Moses (14:12; Exodus 32:10). Once again, Moses, even more fervently than before, interceded on their behalf; he even pleaded for God's own name's sake and His glory and testimony among the heathen nations (14:13-16). In his appeal, after which pardon was granted, Moses quoted God's own words about His merciful and forgiving nature (14:17-19; cf. Exodus 34:6; 20:5-6). It is important to know the Word of God, that we might stand more firmly in our faith and upon His promises.

The Israelites had to pay a grave penalty for their disbelief, but the Lord's judgment was just. Those foolish ones who did not heed Moses' warning disobediently entered the land to fight without the Lord; they suffered the inevitable consequence (14:42-45). Success in spiritual warfare is attained only when the Lord is with us. How tragic that though they were within sight of the Promised Land, they were to turn back to the wilderness where they would remain for forty years, and where death would come upon all those men who had been numbered in the census (14:29-30; 1:45-46), except Caleb and Joshua, whom the Lord blessed and rewarded for their faithfulness.

Prayer for today: O Lord, grant us the courage to move boldly forward with You. May we not lean unto our own understanding, but acknowledge You in all our ways, and You have promised to direct our paths (Proverbs 3:5,6).

Read Numbers 15 & 16 *May 29*

Key Verse: Numbers 16:28 "... *By this you shall know that the Lord has sent me to do all these works, for I have not done them of my own will.*"

After the rebellion at Kadesh (Numbers 14), the people needed to be reminded of the commands of the Lord regarding sacrifices, and to know that these commands were still obligatory, even though they were to remain in the wilderness and would not be entering the Promised Land for forty years. Twice in chapter 15, the Lord reaffirms His intention to give them the land (15:2,18), but it would be their children who would enjoy it; it was these younger people who would need these teachings reaffirmed.

God made provision of atonement for sins committed in ignorance, but it was clearly shown that for deliberate sins committed with evil intent, no sacrifice was acceptable, and that person was to be "completely cut off" (15:31). An example was given of a man stoned to death for despising the command of the Lord concerning the observance of the Sabbath. This may seem harsh, but we must remember these were rebellious people, and it was necessary to strictly enforce the laws or total anarchy would result.

Chapter 15 stresses that the non-Israelite, or stranger who lived among them, was to be welcomed to follow in the ways of the Lord and have fellowship with Him (Romans 3:29). They were, however, also expected to follow the same rules, for God had only one law for both a native-born Israelite and a Gentile (15:14-16, 26, 29-30), that all might enjoy the privileges.

In chapter 16, we read of one of the largest and most well-planned rebellions against Moses. They had not learned from the lesson taught to Aaron and Miriam (Numbers 12). In this conspiracy there were two factions against Moses; (1) A religious revolt that resented the superior rights of the priesthood was led by Korah (a cousin of Moses; Exodus 6:18-21), who was privileged as a Kohathite to assist the priests in an important service of the Tabernacle (4:4). That was not enough for Korah: he coveted the position of the priests. Many of his followers were other overly pious Levites, as well as some men from the general congregation. (2) But there was also a political revolt. Those people resented Moses' leadership and failure to bring them into the Promised Land (they blamed him for God's judgment). This was led by two Reubenites, Dathan and Abiram, who gathered much support from the community by spreading discontent. Both groups united in the uprising and gathered about them 250 influential men of the community. They challenged Moses' authority and charged him with exalting himself over all others whom they said were, "holy, every one of them, and the Lord is among them" (16:3). Moses answered them wisely and challenged them, for only God could make the decision of "who is His and who is holy" (16:5).

The Bible says, concerning God's wrath, "It is a fearful thing to fall into the hands of the living God" (Hebrews 10:31); "For the

Lord will judge His people and have compassion on His servants, when He sees that their power is gone" (Deuteronomy 32:36). In three ways, the Lord vindicated Moses, making the decision clear that he was definitely ordained by Him to be their leader, and only Aaron and his sons, whom He appointed, were to be the priests. (1) God consumed with fire the 250 arrogant men who had joined with Korah, presuming they were worthy to offer incense before Him. Their flattened censers would serve to always remind the people of the cost of rebellion against the Lord and His appointed leaders and priests (16:38). (2) God caused the earth to swallow up Dathan, Abiram, and Korah, along with their household (however, it seems Korah's own sons had not supported him, for later we read that they did not die at that time, Numbers 26:11). (3) After these displays of God's wrath, intended to restore Moses to power and his high position, the Israelites accused him about the severity of the punishments (as though he was the cause). God's anger was once again aroused and a plague began among the people, and before Moses' and Aaron's intercession became effective, nearly 15,000 had died.

Today, many people are in rebellion against God by rejecting His Son Jesus Christ and the authority of His inspired Word, but a great judgment day is coming when all will know the truth and God will show clearly those who are His and those who are not (Matthew 25:31-34, 46).

Prayer for today: *Lord, You are God whom we do fear. You judge sin most harshly. Thank You that You became a human being in the person of Your Son, Jesus, and took the judgment for our sin and rebellion upon Yourself. Grant us the grace and humility to daily recognize and acknowledge this fact before You.*

Read Numbers 17 & 18   *May 30*

Key Verse: Numbers 18:20 *"... You shall have no inheritance in their land...I am your portion and your inheritance among the children of Israel."*

Chapter seventeen continues the challenges of the preceding chapter. It seems the people still needed additional proof of Aaron's authority and rightful position. God vindicated his religious leadership as the high priest by commanding a test that would put an end to all the complaints and show, once and for all, which tribe and priests He had chosen.

As the Lord commanded, the rods (symbols of authority and of their heritage as shepherds) from the head of all the 12 tribes, and one from Aaron representing the Levites, were gathered by Moses and placed overnight in the Most Holy Place before the Ark of the testimony. What happened was something totally supernatural and miraculous, for only Aaron's rod, a piece of dead wood, budded, grew branches, blossomed and produced ripe almonds in a few short hours, and all without any soil, roots, or sunlight!

Nothing is impossible with God. Just as the resurrection of Jesus from the dead attested to His divine commission and authority, so this piece of dead wood, which came alive by the power of God and was transformed into a life-giving branch, attested to Aaron's divine commission and authority. Even people who have been dead in trespasses and sin have been transformed by the power of God from something unlovely and barren into that which is beautiful and fruitful; made alive by the power of Christ (Ephesians 2:1).

What a blessing it must have been for Aaron to see that his rod had budded; a wonderful divine confirmation of his and his tribe's high calling. God had caused his position to be undisputed. To remind and warn the people against rebellion, Aaron's rod was placed in the Most Holy Place.

The reaction of the people was to cry out for mercy (17:12). Did they finally understand they needed someone to draw near to God on their behalf and make atonement for their sins? Now, with the firm establishment of the priesthood, the Lord continued with some general principles concerning sacrifices in His Holy Tabernacle. Since the people now knew the priesthood and the Levitical order were divinely appointed and essential for their own well-being (spiritual and as well as physical, in the protection against divine wrath), they were ready to pay for these services by their offerings, first fruits, and tithes. This is the way the Lord provided for His servants' needs, since they were not to receive any inheritance of the land. The Lord God Himself was their inheritance, for they had a special relationship with Him much more important than wealth and possessions.

The Levites were given as gifts to the priesthood, as well as to all the children of Israel (18:6), and they were to be held responsible if any defilement came upon the Tabernacle. The priests' duties included guarding the Levites from trespassing (18:1). Many laws given before in the book of Leviticus concerning the priests' rights to receive certain portions of the sacrifices, first fruits and first-born clean animals, are now put into a more systematic order. The heave offerings were to be for the priests and their families, "as an ordinance forever; it is a covenant of salt" (18:19), an expression that was used to indicate a perpetual covenant (Leviticus 2:13; 2 Chronicles 13:5; Mark 9:49).

We learn something new here: the tithe belonged to the tribe of Levi for their much needed ministry (18:21). This law would be put into effect upon settlement in the Promised Land, then the Levites in turn would tithe the best of whatever they received to the priesthood (18:26, 29). All the people were to do likewise, for only the best was to be given to God and to His priests (18:12).

The Lord wants His servants, both then and now, to be well provided for by those they serve, having all their needs met, as a "reward" for the service they perform on behalf of the congregation (18:31). Then they are to be good stewards of what has been given to them, for they are "holy gifts", (18:32) since they were given firstly to the Lord, then He gives them to His ministers "as an inheritance" (18:21), for the Lord is their inheritance and as such He is their all-sufficiency.

Prayer for today: *O Lord, we too cry out for mercy. Thank You that Your Word declares that it's not according to our works of righteousness but according to Your mercies You have saved us. (Titus 3:4-5)*

Read Numbers 19 & 20　　*May 31*

Key Verse: **Numbers 20:8** *"Take the rod;... gather the assembly together. Speak to the rock... thus you shall bring water for them out of the rock..."*

The extensive uncleanness that resulted from the plague of judgment (Numbers 16) and the burial of so many bodies at one time required a special ceremony of purification. God, in His wisdom, provided a simple way to purify the Israelites from the defilement caused by contact with the dead; the answer came through the unblemished red heifer. This served as a gracious provision, especially because of the hardships in the wilderness, to make cleansing readily available. Yet if a person defiantly refused to be cleansed, it was very serious, and he was to be "cut off from among the congregation" (19:20).

The red heifer was not a sacrificial animal, but one through which ceremonial cleansing was provided. It was to be slaughtered, not sacrificed; killed outside the camp, and not at the altar. It was to be totally burned, all at one time with cedar wood, hyssop, and some scarlet cloth (symbols of purification). The blood was also burned with it, except for a small amount taken by the priest, Eleazar, to sprinkle with his finger "seven times directly in front of the tabernacle" (19:4).

The ashes were of primary importance, for when ordinary water was mixed with them, it became the water of purification. "For if the...ashes of a heifer...sanctifies for the purifying of the flesh, how much more shall the blood of Christ...purge your conscience from dead works to serve the living God?" (Hebrews 9:13-14).

We are not told the year in which the events of chapter 20 took place, but if we compare chapter 33:38, we are led to conclude that it was the fortieth year after the exodus from Egypt, meaning that it was the people of the second generation who, in just one more year, would be entering the Promised Land.

Here we read of the death of Miriam and Aaron; both died within a short time of each other (Moses death was not very long afterward, Deuteronomy 32:49-50). It seems God told Aaron in advance of his forthcoming death and, in preparation, his high priestly robes were passed on to his son, Eleazar (20:28), showing that although Aaron died, the priesthood remained.

Like their fathers before them, this generation was prone to complain, this time about the water shortage. In another place, forty years before, God had miraculously supplied water from a rock and on this first occasion Moses had been told to strike the rock with his rod (Exodus 17:5-6). On this second occasion, when God told Moses He would do a similar miracle, Moses was only to "speak to the rock" and the water would come forth (20:8). This time Moses disobeyed God: He lost his temper and patience at the complaining crowd of "rebels". Although he was most meek (12:3), he did have human weaknesses, something which the inspired Word of God does not hide about its heroes. So Moses spoke to the people, not to the rock; he and Aaron did not give God the credit and glory ("must **we** bring water...?") and in anger he struck the rock twice (20:10-11). Even though God disapproved of the means, He was faithful to His word and did indeed supernaturally provide the water from the rock. Moses' actions, however, marred the holy image of God and His punishment was alike for both brothers. Sadly, neither would be permitted to enter the Promised Land (20:12). Moses' hopes and dreams, since the time he had left Egypt, were to joyously lead the people of God into the land; now, because of his sin, that dream was shattered. God did allow him to see the land from the mountain where he died (Deuteronomy 34:4-5), and, much later, to visit the land at the time of Jesus' transfiguration (Matthew 17:3).

A further difficult time that Moses faced shortly thereafter was with Edom. Probably desiring to arouse sympathy, he called the Israelites Edom's "brother" (20:14), since the Edomites were descendants of Esau, Jacob's (Israel's) brother. However, their plea to pass through Edom's territory was strongly rejected, even to the point of Edom sending soldiers to guard their border, thus forcing Israel to make a more difficult journey of an extra fifty or sixty kilometers through the hot, barren desert. Israel's prophets frequently denounced Edom's many acts of hatred toward Israel, and the end result was God's judgment of destruction (Ezekiel 35:5,11; Obadiah 10).

Prayer for today: *Almighty God, we worship You for Your great and mighty acts of mercy to a rebellious and complaining human family. Grant us the grace to listen carefully to all Your Word and to carry out Your instructions for our lives.*

YEAR ONE
SPRING

JUNE

Among the ruins of ancient Capernaum is found this relief of the Holy Ark of the Covenant hewn in stone.

Special Note: Be sure to write in your request NOW for your next volume of DAY UNTO DAY, *Year One – Summer* edition. It starts July 1!

Read Numbers 21 *June 1*

Key Verse: Numbers 21:8 *"...Make a fiery serpent, and set it on a pole; and it shall be that everyone who is bitten, when he looks at it, shall live."*

Since the Israelites were not allowed to pass through Edom (20:21), their journey took them southward through a difficult territory full of enemies. One of these enemies, Arad the Canaanite, took some Israelites captive. This unexpected trial caused Israel to turn to God, indicate their dependence upon Him, and make a vow to Him. God honoured them with a great victory, the first taste of victory for this new generation of Israelites.

Though they must have been encouraged with their first victory, the long, hard journey around Edom soon led to frustration and discouragement. In obedience to God, Moses had refused to allow the Israelites to pass through Edom and engage in battle with them, for God had given that land to Esau (Deuteronomy 2:4-6). Because of their first victory, they were probably confident in themselves of another. Had they forgotten that the victory over Arad was only because God had granted it, and that previously they had been defeated because of going into battle in disobedience to Him (14:41-45)? Impatient with Moses and the direction the Lord was leading, they, like their fathers, began complaining about being led into the wilderness to die, when actually God had been sustaining them. Their most bitter complaint, and a very serious offense, was despising the heavenly manna, thus spurning God's gracious provision.

Although God is longsuffering and patient, their complaints and contemptuous behaviour provoked His wrath, resulting in the plague of poisonous snakes that caused many deaths. The Apostle Paul used this incident as a warning for us to learn from their example (1 Corinthians 10:9-11). Finally, in recognition of their sin, the people came to repentance (21:7), and God made a gracious provision for healing through the bronze serpent that Moses was to lift up. Two things were required for healing and life: (1) the serpent had to be looked upon in **faith** and belief that God could heal; (2) each individual bitten had to personally look upon it with his own eyes. This clearly forepictured salvation by faith, for likewise we can look to the cross of Jesus Christ and receive healing, salvation, and eternal life (John 3:14-16; Isaiah 53:4-5). For the Israelites, it was not the object itself that brought the healing; it was their faith in God. However, later in the history of Israel we see that the bronze serpent became an object of cultic worship which the godly king Hezekiah had to destroy to show that it was only faith and trust in God, not any object, that brought healing (2 Kings 18:4).

After seeing the Lord's salvation from the fatal snake bites, the Israelites moved under the guidance of the Lord in a north-easterly direction until they came to the plains of Moab. It must have thrilled Moses' heart to hear the people singing joyously as they travelled, instead of always complaining (21:17-18).

As with Edom, the Israelites sent a cordial message to Sihon, king of Ammon, asking permission to peacefully pass through their territory. Moses did not want to engage in war with those who were descendants of Lot (Abraham's nephew), however, conflict was unavoidable, for Sihon attacked Israel but was defeated. How encouraged Israel must have been to defeat those who had defeated Moab. A similar victory was won over Og, the king of Bashan, after the Lord had told Moses not to fear him. With this victory, the region east of the Jordan was controlled by Israel. These victories caused the men of Jericho to fear the Israelites (Joshua 2:10) who were greatly encouraged and praised God (Psalm 135:9-12; 136:17-22). Similarly, every victory and spiritual success in the life of a believer should encourage him to walk even closer to God, being more confident in His strength and expecting greater things to come.

Prayer for today: O Lord, we praise You for Your mighty works. Grant us the faith to look to Jesus who was lifted up on the Cross. We claim Your promise that this looking unto Jesus will bring healing and deliverance.

Read Numbers 22 & 23 *June 2*

Key Verse: Numbers 22:12 *"And God said to Balaam, "You shall not go with them; you shall not curse the people, for they are blessed."*

Balak, the pagan king of Moab, undoubtedly heard of Israel's other victories and became terrified that they might attack him. He knew that in order to defeat Israel he needed supernatural help; therefore he called upon the well-known heathen soothsayer, Balaam, to pronounce a curse upon them, and in return Balaam would be well paid. The nomadic Midianites, who were allies of the Moabites, had probably heard of Balaam's fame in their travels and reported it to Balak, who would have believed in magical divination. Some nobles of Moab and Midian were sent on a long journey to bring Balaam from northern Mesopotamia, about 450 kilometers away. Was he a true prophet of God? Some of his words might lead one to believe he was, but he probably considered himself the spokesman for any god. The Hebrew text does not call him the title of "nabi", meaning a prophet, but rather "kosem", a soothsayer (Joshua 13:22), and such people were not to be tolerated, for they were "an abomination to the Lord" (Deuteronomy 18:10-12).

No one can dispute that God actually spoke to Balaam; He clearly told him not to go for the purpose of cursing Israel (22:12). However, when a second delegation of a higher status came, promising even more wealth to Balaam, he asked them to wait until he heard from God, probably hoping that He would change His mind; however Balaam himself later uttered words in his first oracle expressing God's immutability (23:19). There was no need to wait for God's answer, since He had already said "no". However, because God knows the heart and will of man, He allowed Balaam to go because of Balaam's own will, but stipulated that he only speak the words He gave him. On Balaam's journey, God clearly showed His displeasure with him, for it would seem Balaam inwardly desired to curse Israel, in disobedience to God.

With his hard heart, Balaam was blinded from seeing the angel of God armed with a sword; however his donkey was not, and its reactions on the three different occasions of the angel's appearance made Balaam furious and he struck it. The well-known miracle of Balaam's donkey speaking then took place, but even its rebuke of Balaam did not deter him from his desire to proceed. Finally, God opened his eyes to see the angel, and Balaam acted like a penitent, but it seems it wasn't true repentance from the heart. The angel allowed him to pass, but strongly warned him again to speak only the words God gave him (22:35), thus making him more aware of the seriousness of what he was to do, for he was not to change the word of God.

Even though he spoke the true words of God, they are not referred to as a prophecy, but rather they are called by the more appropriate term, "oracle" (23:7). Balaam was but a vehicle through whom God spoke, just as the donkey was a vehicle through which God rebuked Balaam. Balaam, who had wanted to curse Israel, was made to bless them because of God's love for them (Deuteronomy 23:5). Although Balaam expressed the desire to be like the Israelites (23:10b), his heart was not right, for he certainly did not die in peaceful righteousness (Joshua 13:22).

God gave Balaam two oracles of blessing that were truths from God: the first was about Israel's being separate from the other nations and that they would be as numerous as the dust (23:9-10); the second was about the faithfulness and unchanging character of God, Israel's purity, and His promise that no divination could harm God's defence over His people, and that they would be victorious (23:19-24).

Balaam, himself a sorcerer and brought by Balak for the express purpose of magically cursing the Israelites, had to admit in his oracle that "there is no sorcery against Jacob, nor is there any divination against Israel" (23:23). He was rendered powerless by God to do or say anything evil against Israel as Balak had desired. Likewise, we as believers covered by the blood of Jesus are protected from any harmful, direct attacks against us by the enemy, as is the Church as a whole, and "the gates of Hades shall not prevail against it" (Matthew 16:18b).

Prayer for today: *Lord God of Israel, thank You that You deliver from all power of sorcery. Thank You that you turn curses into blessings for Your children.*

Read Numbers 24 & 25   *June 3*

Key Verse: Numbers 25:12,13 *"...Behold, I give to him My covenant of peace...because he was zealous for his God, and made atonement for...Israel."*

Here we see the third and final desperate attempt of Balak to get Balaam to curse Israel. Once again, Balak took him to a different place in hopes that the place would make the difference and that from there Balaam would be able to curse them. For the third time they again sacrificed upon seven altars, but here we learn that Balaam "did not seek to use sorcery" (24:1) as he had before — he knew it was of no avail.

The ancient sorcerers would seek for omens in the livers and organs of the animals that were offered to the gods (in this case Baal of Peor). The One and only true God of Israel would never reveal Himself through such an abomination; rather, His Spirit came upon Balaam who was but an instrument to speak His truth. This was by no means an infilling, for it was only temporary; God's Spirit was only upon him but not within him, as He was with true men of God (27:18). Balaam was faithful in his calling to be a spokesman for any deity, so He did speak truly the words God gave him. Surely, because of the angel's strong warning, Balaam was afraid to do otherwise. Yet his heart and motivation were wrong, and though he could not curse Israel and thereby not receive "honour" from Balak (i.e. tangible honour, namely riches; 24:11), it seems he looked for another way to make his long journey worthwhile.

Much to Balak's displeasure, Balaam's third oracle was yet another blessing, describing the beauty of Israel, their coming exaltation and victory, and finally repeating the promise God had given to

Abraham (24:9; cf. Genesis 12:3). For Balak, this was the last straw. In extreme anger, he fired Balaam without pay (24:11), but Balaam was not quite finished; the most beautiful oracle was yet to come. Each successive oracle had brought a higher revelation, and until this point in Scripture, the fourth oracle brought the fullest revelation of the Messiah: "A Star shall come out of Jacob; a Scepter shall rise out of Israel...Out of Jacob One shall have dominion" (24:17, 19; cf. Revelation 22:16; Genesis 49:10). Then Balaam continued to foretell the disaster that would befall those nations which had desired to see Israel cursed (24:20-22).

Although the story is not told, we can imply from later references that Balaam did not depart for his home immediately after the fourth oracle (24:25; 31:8), but rather remained among the Midianites and suggested to them means whereby Israel could come to destruction: by leading them into idolatry and immorality (31:16; Revelation 2:14). He knew it was impossible to curse that which God had blessed, but he also knew the Holy God of Israel would not tolerate sin. Balaam's advice was followed and their evil scheme against Israel worked. However, Midian later suffered the penalty for their participation in the seduction of Israel (25:17-18; chapter 31).

We read here of the last rebellion and divine judgment of Israel during the wilderness experience. It was while they were at their final encampment on the eastern side of the Jordan river before entering the Promised Land. Satan's schemes are deceptive, for Midian's friendship and Israel's compromise with them brought Israel greater problems than would a conflict. They broke the covenant with their God as they succumbed to the evil seduction of the Midianite women who led many astray into idolatry and fornication. Those Israelites who led the wickedness were killed and put on public display to warn others of the consequences of sin. Many others died by a plague sent by God which would have consumed them all if not for the brave, holy zeal of Phinehas which stopped God's wrath (25:7-8,11; Psalm 106:28-32) and seemingly awakened the people to realize the depth of sin into which they had fallen. It is tragic that by the end of God's judgment a total of 24,000 had died. God blessed and honoured Phinehas because of his faithfulness (the Lord will honour those who honour Him, 1 Samuel 2:30) and promised him His "covenant of peace", and from his family (Aaron's line) was to come Israel's high priests. The true and final High Priest, whom all the high priests symbolized, is Jesus Christ, who brought into fulfilment the promised covenant of peace (Hebrews 7:21-25).

Prayer for today: *O Lord, when the schemes of the enemy come against us, deliver us. Keep us from the trap of compromise with the world and its' sinful ways.*

Read Numbers 26 & 27 June 4

Key Verse: Numbers 27:16-17 *"Let the Lord...set a man over the congregation, that [they] may not be like sheep which have no shepherd."*

The time was coming closer for the entrance into the Promised Land by the new generation; therefore another census was required. This one was more detailed than the first census, since it included the names of all the heads of the families within each tribe. It not only counted the fighting men age twenty and upward, but provided a basis for dividing the land which God was soon to give them. The size of the tribe would indicate how much land they would inherit, but the placing of the tribes was to be decided by casting lots, a common method used in those days whereby they believed God to intervene in determining the outcome (26:54-56).

During the course of the enumeration, we are reminded of the sad incident regarding the sinful rebellion of Korah and the Reubenites, Dathan, and Abiram (26:9-10), a judgment which caused many deaths in the tribe of Reuben (probably the reason their numbers were down in this census), as well as deaths in the other tribes; and we again read of the deaths of Nadab and Abihu (26:61). These incidents would serve as a reminder for the new generation not to take the commands of God lightly.

Though they were in their fortieth year since leaving Egypt, the Israelites were now a little less in number (compare 1:46; 26:51) due to the hardship of the wilderness life, but mainly due to the many judgments of God for their wickedness. For those who fear (honour and respect) God, He is merciful, but He is also just and all His punishments were justly deserved. The Lord showed grace and favour to Joshua and Caleb, the only two fighting men of the first census who remained faithful to Him (14:29-30).

With the census and the coming division of the land, five daughters of a man who had died without a son courageously came before Moses, Eleazer, and the elders. They were concerned about their father's name being left out among those who would receive an inheritance, as well as their own rights of inheritance. Moses took the matter up with God, and He quickly gave them a favourable response (27:7). With this, God elevated the position of women and, in fact, wherever the Bible has been honoured, the position of women has been lifted up.

The time was coming soon for possession of the Promised Land, but that also meant the approaching death of Moses, since the punishment for his sin at the waters of Meribah was his exclusion from entering the land (27:14; 20:12). This seems harsh, but it serves as a warning to spiritual leaders of the seriousness of their calling and the great responsibilities they have to glorify God in all things and at all times.

Moses' prayer reflects the true heart of this great man of God, one who dearly loved his people. Before he died, Moses wisely asked God to choose his successor (for God's choice would be the best) that they might not be without a shepherd (27:17). His compassionate concern for the people was similar to that of the great coming Prophet, Priest, and King (Matthew 9:36), as was his humble attitude of putting aside his personal desires to see the best for those to whom he was called to serve (a mark of a true leader; Hebrews 3:5). God did indeed answer Moses' prayer with His faithful servant Joshua. To be a leader, one must first be a servant (Matthew 20:25-28).

Joshua was set in front of the whole congregation to show that he was God's choice and had Moses' support. The laying on of hands symbolized the transferring of authority, honour and responsibility from Moses to Joshua, so that he would have the same respect and obedience of the people. However, Moses' office of prophet was not transferred since he alone had that special place with God wherein he could go before the Lord and speak directly with Him. To receive guidance from the Lord, Joshua would have to go through Eleazar the high priest, who would in turn look for God's will and guidance in the "Urim" (see Exodus 28:30).

Prayer for today: *Lord God, we praise You for Your constant involvement in human affairs. Because You care so passionately, we can trust You to give godly leadership. May we humbly respect Your choices for leadership in Your cause.*

Read Numbers 28 & 29   *June 5*

Key Verse: Numbers 28:2 *"Command the children of Israel...My offerings...you shall be careful to offer to Me at their appointed time."*

In these two chapters, the calendar for the whole religious year is described. It is similar to Leviticus 23, but here we find stressed the definite quantities of the offerings and the exact dates for each occasion. The priests were to carefully observe these on behalf of the whole nation.

It appears that during the time of the wilderness wanderings, because of adverse conditions, many of the regular sacrificial laws had been suspended. At this point in their history, when they were to become settled in the Promised Land and able to fulfil these laws, the reaffirmation of these laws was necessary. Also, even though Joshua was soon to replace Moses as leader, everyone was to know that the laws God had given through Moses were still binding.

There were to be continual, regular sacrifices daily, weekly (on the Sabbath), monthly (at the beginning of each new month), and yearly (the 7 great annual feasts). The priests were kept busy with continuous activity unto the Lord. Theirs was an enormous task. We today, as the priests of God, likewise need to devote our time to Him and keep busy in the calling He has for us in His service. The the believer's task today is equally enormous: telling the world of God's grace and love through His son, Jesus. Rest and relaxation is necessary, but idleness is not.

The Lord God described His offerings as "My food" (28:2). Offerings went up to God in smoke upon the altar as a "sweet aroma" to the Lord, for they expressed devotion and obedience to Him and caused Him to see the offerer as acceptable in His sight. Just as we require food at certain times in the course of the day, so God requires of us to give Him regular and continuous expressions of our love and devotion.

The twenty-ninth chapter deals with the festivals in the very busy seventh month, a month containing more solemn feasts than any other month (Trumpets, Day of Atonement, and Tabernacles). Only here do we read of the offerings for the eight days of the Feast of Tabernacles. These and the other offerings we read of were requirements in addition to the vow and freewill offerings (29:39). The Lord took much pleasure in what was done over and above the basic requirements.

The priests' activities would always remind the people of their spiritual needs. In fact, the whole year and the life of the community was built around these sacred times. Especially stressed is the burnt offering which was to be offered two times daily as a sweet aroma to the Lord (28:3,6), expressing dedication, surrender and communion with Him. These regular offerings would keep the people aware of their covenant relationship with God and the importance of continual communion with Him made possible by the sin offerings.

Those in the covenant relationship with God today must never neglect to devote time to Him every day by prayer and reading His word. This wonderful fellowship with God was made possible by the one Sin Offering of Jesus that never again needs to be repeated. It is striking to read of the great numbers of animals required as sacrifices, yet this was because they were insufficient. It helps us to realize all the more the significance of the great, all-sufficent, perfect, and ultimate sacrifice of our Lord Jesus Christ, who willingly gave Himself upon the altar of the cross. His blood alone, shed once and for all, can make atonement for our sins today.

Prayer for today: *Thank You Lord for the great privilege of prayer. Help us never to take this for granted, but to value our access to You most highly.*

Read Numbers 30 & 31 *June 6*

Key verse: Numbers 31:49 *"... Your servants have taken a count of the men of war who are under our command, and not a man of us is missing."*

Chapter thirty is the only Old Testament passage dealing with women's vows. It begins by speaking of a man's vow which was very solemn and binding (30:2). Upon entrance into the Promised Land, many people would surely make a vow of some of their substance in gratitude to the Lord. Therefore, they were strongly cautioned here that it was very serious, for "it is better not to vow than to vow and not pay" (Ecclesiastes 5:2-5).

Women who were either still in their father's households or who had a husband were to come under that man's authority, and if she made a vow it was only binding if her father or husband agreed. A vow of a widowed or a divorced woman, however, was binding like a man's.

These laws were given for the welfare of the family, showing the importance of unity within the home, for many disputes could arise if there was an uncertain order of authority. Even the New Testament teaches that the husband is to be the head of the home. This does not lower the position of women, but clarifies the responsibilities within the home. When these divinely given guidelines are followed, there is much more peacefulness within a home. Strife could arise in a family if an Israelite woman made a rash vow involving a large sum of money or land, for it was really the father or husband, as the main bread-winner of the family, who would, in the end, be responsible to pay it. For this reason, her vow was only validated if he gave it his blessing, but if he did not, he would be responsible to bear the guilt, meaning he would be obliged to meet all the ceremonial and legal requirements involved in the sin of breaking a vow, as though it were his own.

In chapter thirty-one, we read of Moses' final involvement in a holy war, and it was against the Midianites (31:2). They were descendants of Abraham (Genesis 25:1-2) but had lost any knowledge of the true God and were idolatrous pagans. They (with the advice of Balaam) had been responsibe for scheming the seduction of the Israelites who fell into terrible sin and "played the harlot" by idolatry and immorality, wherein 24,000 had died due to God's. judgment (25:9). God therefore judged Midian, ordering Israel to take vengeance upon them. With the Lord before them, represented by Phinehas the priest and the holy articles and led by the trumpeter (31:6; 10:9), the 12,000 soldiers went to war and had a tremendous victory. There was not even one Israelite fatality (31:49), but every Midianite on the battleground was killed, including the five kings and Balaam the sorcerer (31:7-8). The soldiers all realized this was because the Lord was with them and, out of gratitude, they all contributed and brought an enormous offering (31:50-52). The amount of spoil taken from the Midianites was amazing; it not only enriched the soldiers, but all the people and the Tabernacle as well. King David later used these guidelines as a permanent ordinance in Israel (1 Samuel 30:24-25).

Among the spoil were women and children. Moses was enraged to see the immoral women who had led in Israel's seduction and ordered them killed along with all the boys. Only the virgin girls were spared. This seems extremely harsh and cruel to us, but we are living in a different day and age, and we must understand that God had reasons. His ways are often beyond our comprehension, but we can be confident that He is just. If the women had been allowed to live among them, the Israelites could have again been easily led into corruption. If the boys had been allowed to live among them, they could have taken the rightful inheritance of the land that God was giving only to the children of Israel.

Everything that came back after having contact with the Midianites required ceremonial cleansing, be it the soldiers, or the spoil (31:19-24). Contact with sin is contaminating, and God, required that there be no compromise for his children with the sinful things of this world. He requires that of us today, too. Uncleanness prevents quality communion with Him.

Prayer for today: *O Lord, we do not understand all Your ways, but we do understand that You hate sin and will never become tolerant of it. In Your mercy, Lord, You sent Your Son Jesus to save us from our sins as You promised to do in the word spoken by the Angel about His birth.*

Read Numbers 32 *June 7*

Key Verse: Numbers 32:23 *"But if you do not do so, then take note, you have sinned against the Lord; and be sure your sin will find you out."*

With the defeat of Midian, the Israelites acquired much additional livestock and land that was fertile and favourable for grazing (31:32-34). Rather than crossing the Jordan, the tribes of Reuben and Gad desired to settle in these areas, but this was not God's plan. He had given all the tribes their inheritance on the other side of the Jordan and their placement was to be determined by God through the casting of lots.

Moses' initial reaction to Reuben and Gad was anger. He was afraid that their request would influence the others to remain complacent with what they had already received, rather than going on into Canaan where they would have to face unknown enemies. He related their request with the tragedy at Kadesh many year previous which resulted in their fathers discouraging the people from entering the Promised Land and the rebellion which led to God's judgment (Numbers 14). The tribes reassurred Moses that their request was not an act of rebellion but that all their fighting men would wholeheartedly support them in the battle on the other side of the Jordan, though their families and livestock would remain.

With their persistence and this vow, Moses consented, although we do not read of his seeking the Lord's guidance beforehand as he usually did with important decisions. He strongly warned the tribes of Gad and Reuben to be true to their words, for to break them would be a sin and God would surely know (32:23), implying divine wrath would come upon them for lying to him and God. The records show they remained true to their word and sent their soldiers across in battle, along with those of the half tribe of Manasseh (Joshua 4:12; 22:1-4), who probably decided to remain with them in Transjordan when they saw the others had permission.

After Moses' consent, these tribes quickly went to work rebuilding and renaming those Midianite cities which had been burned. It was not God's intention that any Israelite settle outside of the Promised Land; however, these tribes settled for second best, shunning God's gracious gift, and in so doing they missed His blessing. It also showed a disregard for His will, because they put their own will first. History proved that Moses' consent for them to remain in Transjordan brought many problems, for when man's worldly choices come before God's, it hinders His purpose and leads to trouble. Soon after Israel had settled in the Promised Land, conflict and misunderstanding arose between those on the God-given west side of the Jordan and those on the east (Joshua 22). The tribes of Reuben, Gad and half of Mannaseh were not only separated geographically from the rest of the tribes, but separated in that they lacked the unity they once had. This afforded them less protection in time of war; they were the first tribes to be taken into captivity (2 Kings 17; 1 Chronicles 5:26) . They were far removed from the Tabernacle and temple worship, so they lacked the proper fellowship which was detrimental to their spirituality. In the time of Jesus, these descendants of Israel had long since lost all claim to the promises of God through Abraham and were spiritually apostate.

We learn from this chapter that it is better to be in the centre of God's will than to make our own choices out of a selfish desire and pay the sad consequences. Blessings follow those that follow the Lord. Our God knows all things, including our motivations. Sin against the Lord never goes unnoticed, for indeed "your sin will find you out". In one way or another, our sins will be exposed (judgment day), but "If we confess our sins, He is faithful and just to forgive us our sins and to cleanse us from all unrighteousness" (1 John 1:9).

Prayer for today: *O Lord, please keep us from making short-sighted and selfish choices which could keep us from doing Your perfect will throughout the rest of our lives.*

Read Numbers 33 & 34   June 8

Key Verse: Numbers 33:51-52 *"When you have crossed the Jordan... you shall drive out all the inhabitants... destroy all their engraved stones, ... molded images, and ... high places."*

The Lord commanded Moses to write down all the places Israel had set up camp from the time they left Egypt until they entered the Promised Land (attests to the Mosaic authorship, 33:2). There are forty places mentioned, which would mean the average stay at each encampment was one year. The Israelites had been forced to live like nomads ever since the time they had rebelled against God (14:33). They had moved from place to place according to the grazing needs of their livestock, the need for water, safety, and the weather conditions.

Most of the new generation would not remember the earlier places of their parents' wanderings. This list would show them exactly where they had travelled and make their punishment for sin all the more clear. However, it would also show them how God had blessed and sustained them throughout all those years (see Deuteronomy 2:7), just as God walks with and sustains His people today. There is no mention of the sins the people had committed at the various places, for the past was to be put behind them, as they were about to enter into a new stage of their history and were to look to the future.

God gave them specific commands for the future conquest of Canaan — a conquest which was by divine appointment and would be brought about by the power of God alone. When they entered the land, they were to completely destroy anything that had to do with the pagan religion of the Canaanites and drive them all out of the land. This was necessary for the spiritual welfare of Israel, for they were weak and had previously fallen easily into idolatry. God warned Israel that if they did not do this, the Canaanites would be a continuous source of adversity and He would punish them in the same way he had planned for the Canaanites (33:55-56). History shows that Israel failed to heed these warnings and fell into terrible sin for which they were indeed punished, especially with the Assyrian and Babylonian captivities. From these warnings, we learn that if the Lord's people are to remain pure and holy before Him, they must first remove everything from their lives which does not glorify and please Him.

Chapter thirty-four continues with further instructions for the future. God shared with Moses the specific borders of the Promised Land. They are given as evidence of His great gift to His people. Their southern border was to be along the land of Edom, from the southern tip of the Dead Sea up to the Mediterranean Sea; on the west, the coastline of the Mediterranean Sea; on the north, the area of the Mount Hermon range; and on the east, the Jordan valley from the Sea of Galilee to the Dead Sea.

We also read here the names of the newly appointed tribal leaders who were to assist Joshua and Eleazar, the priest, in the dividing of the land as the Lord had directed (Joshua 15). These were preparatory steps of faith which showed a trust in God for the successful possession of the land of Canaan. We can observe that among the names listed there is not one which had been mentioned among the first choosing of tribal leaders (chapter one), for all of them had died in the wilderness, nor are any of these a son of a former leader who had led the people in rebellion. Of the former generation, only two had remained faithful, and therefore God raised them to leadership positions: Joshua over all the people and Caleb over the important and large tribe of Judah.

Faithfulness has its rewards, but there is a price to pay for disobedience, and the Israelites paid dearly. Sadly, because of their sin, the full extent of the borders that God had described were never realized, except for a short period of time during the reigns of King David and Solomon.

Prayer for today: *Heavenly Father, we praise You for Your promises to us. Grant that we may not fail in this New Covenant age to meet Your condition for the fulfilment of all Your promises to us.*

Read Numbers 35 & 36 *June 9*

Key Verse: Numbers 35:34 *"Therefore do not defile the land which you inhabit, . . . for I the Lord dwell among the children of Israel."*

Since the Levites were not to receive any inheritance of land like the other tribes, God made provision for them with the allotment of forty-eight cities scattered throughout the land wherein they could live with their families. They were also to receive land surrounding each of the cities for their livestock. In Joshua chapter twenty-one, we read of the fulfilment of this command that the Lord gave to Moses, even though Moses Himself would not live to see it. The reason behind this command was probably to keep a spiritual influence felt in all the land.

Six of the forty-eight cities were to be designated as "cities of refuge". This was a gracious provision from God to protect a suspected murderer from the "avenger" until he could come to a fair trial (35:12). A close relative of the deceased was expected to take upon himself the responsibility for avenging the blood of his kinsmen. This would prevent large family feuds that might cause the unneccessary deaths of several. The same person who was the blood avenger was also to be the kinsman redeemer. He would redeem, or buy back, a relative sold into slavery, or redeem a lost inheritance of his kinsmen. All this would be done to maintain the honour of the family.

If the death was found to be accidental, the slayer could flee for safety to one of the cities of refuge. These were located strategically throughout the land so that one could be reached within a short period of time. God graciously allowed for three of the cities to be located in Transjordan to protect those who had remained there; the other three were in the land of Canaan. Though a death might have been caused unintentionally, the slayer had still spilt a man's blood and was to remain in the city of refuge, for if he left he was fair game for the avenger of blood. However, upon the death of the high priest, he was granted pardon and could safely return to his home, and any avenging would be unlawful. If the slayer was found guilty of wilful murder by using a hard item or weapon (35:16-18), with the testimony of more than one witness he was to be put to death by the avenger of blood and not afforded any protection.

With these laws and others, Israel had the highest form of justice compared with their heathen neighbours. They had a high regard for the sanctity of life, since they knew they had been made in God's image. It was such a serious thing to kill and shed the blood of a man that it would bring defilement upon the land; and the land in which the Lord dwelt was to remain pure. They were to respect God, and other people as well.

The last chapter of the book of Numbers wraps up the account of the five brotherless daughters of Zelophehad (27:1-11). The men of their tribe were considering the ramifications of the women's rights to the inheritance. What would happen if they married outside of the tribe? The land would then be lost to its original inheritors. Moses again sought the Lord's answer; He responded that if any woman became an heiress, she was obliged to marry a man from within her own tribe, so the family allotments would not "change hands from one tribe to another" (36:9). We read that the noble daughters of Zelophehad did as the Lord commanded. Considering all the occasions of disobedience in the Book of Numbers, this is a happy note upon which to end.

Prayer for today: *We flee unto You for refuge, O God. Thank You for Your provision of a safe place in Jesus where we fear no evil.*

Introduction to
The Book of John

The Gospel of John is a good balance to the Gospel of Luke. Why? Simply because the objective perspective of the historian Luke is balanced by the subjective warmth of the personal friend, John. Wilbert F. Howard says in his introduction to John that, "The Gospel [according to John] is in many ways the crown of the Scriptures. It is the simplest and at the same time the most profound book in the New Testament. History and interpretation, biography and theology, are blended in such a way that the reader, seeing the Jesus of history, yet sees Him in the light of Christian experience." (Interpreter's Bible, Vol.8, p.437).

Although there is this subjective warmth there is also a serious theological message in John. His purpose is, "that you may believe that Jesus is the Christ, the Son of God, and that believing you may have life in His name" (20:31). This Gospel is focussed on the truth — the truth as the Truth.

Two key words in John are "life" and "light". He speaks of Jesus as the light of the world bringing eternal life to all who believe on Him. Many of the miracles and teachings of Jesus that John chooses to highlight underscore this light and life imagery.

Other key words are "truth" and "love". It is John who stresses Jesus as the personification of truth and the view of God as "love".

Perhaps the key chapter in John, and maybe in the entire New Testament, is chapter three. More people have embraced Christ because of this chapter than any other single chapter in the Bible. And the key verse in this key chapter is John 3:16, "For God so loved the world, that He gave His only begotten Son, that whosoever believeth on Him, shall not perish, but have everlasting life."

Read John 1 *June 10*

Key Verse: John 1:18 (NIV) *"No one has ever seen God, but God the One and Only, who is at the Father's side, has made Him known."*

I was riding the commuter train the other day and overheard a conversation between two college students sitting behind me. They were dismissing Christianity as untrustworthy because, "Noah's ark was a fable. And the Bible was written by a bunch of guys we don't know. How do we know if their writings weren't the result of some drug-induced hallucination?" They were quite cordial about all this. Their conversation finally eroded to a discussion of the humour of Bill Cosby. As I left the train at my stop, I watched them disappear into the horizon, painlessly unbelieving, arranging for a "burger and a movie" the next Saturday night.

They think doubt about authors and an ark is a problem? They should try this on for size: "only God sees God as He sits beside Himself". That's what I've written in the margin of my Bible beside John 1:18. Somebody on drugs here? Sometimes you'd think so. So much of the Bible (especially what it says about Christ's divinity) is so far beyond reason that one can at least empathize with those who reduce it all to hallucinatory imaginings: unless it's true.

Unless it's true. If it's true, then we have the authoritative Word of God on the subjects of God Himself, Jesus, the kingdom of Heaven, creation, and the end of days. If Jesus was God, then we have confidence in some of the difficult passages in the Old Testament, because Jesus so often quoted and expressed the highest view of those Jewish Scriptures. In fact, He saw Himself as the fulfillment of "Moses and the Prophets". If Jesus was trustworthy then the Scriptures become trustworthy — and even if we may have no "experience" or facility with some of the "unreasonable" aspects of Scripture, we nevertheless rest confident that Jesus knew and understood all of "Holy Writ".

One day, in heaven, we'll all go to school and get the full scoop on the knotty problems of the Bible, but I must stress again that our trust of the Bible is predicated on our trust in Jesus. The word is predicated on the Word. And because that Word became flesh and gave us the "word", we believe and hope. In fact, I might go so far as to say my religion is predicated on relationship. Relationship with Jesus.

Prayer for Today: *Thank you, Father, for sending the Word, clothed in human flesh, bringing light to the darkness. May we be bright bearers of that light.*

Read John 2 & 3 — *June 11*

Key Verse: John 3:3 *"...unless one is born again, he cannot see the kingdom of God."*

Have you ever been challenged to explain what you mean by the term, when you refer to yourself, or to someone else, as a "born-again" Christian? Maybe you've found it a bit difficult to say what you mean. If I can be so presumptuous, allow me to suggest what you mean!

You mean that the kingdom of God is a spiritual reality — unseen except with newly-born eyes. Your physical eyes won't do. Although, ironically, as useless as your natural eyes are, you can't have spiritual eyes until you have physical eyes. That's why you've got to be naturally born ("of water..") before you can be spiritually born ("...and the Spirit.." — v.5). First flesh, then spirit. Jesus doesn't relate to disembodied spirits in the human realm. You've got to have a body, both now ("au naturel") and in eternity ("au glorified").

You also mean that this spiritual birth is affected by the Holy Spirit — God Himself. "Spirit gives birth to spirit", Jesus says. It's only at the initiative of the Spirit that any mere human spirit even considers, let alone commits itself to, coming to Christ.

That's right — I've just introduced a new ingredient: "coming to Christ". Being "born again" is meaningless without belief in and commitment to Christ. "The Son of Man must be lifted up" on the cross so that all men and women throughout history can see Him and decide. If the decision is to believe, then the believer "may have eternal life".

Finally, you mean that you've beem born to a new life that is eternally inviolable — no one can take it away from you. Not that the forces of evil won't try to wrest it from you, or if that fails, to erode it from you casually and seemingly imperceptibly. But, in being born again you've been "saved" from destruction. When Satan counts his victims you won't be among them. You've entered a new life.

Prayer for Today: *Lord, give us today the full assurance of having been "born again". We sometimes need reminding that "old things have passed away and behold all things have become new" (2 Corinthians 5:17).*

Read John 4 — *June 12*

Key Verse: John 4:24 *"God is Spirit, and those who worship Him must worship in spirit and truth."*

I love this story. For several reasons. First, because Jesus was such a free spirit that He had no qualms about talking to a woman on equal ground. That ground, in this case, was at Jacob's well near Sychar in Samaria. But what made it even more astonishing, as far as onlookers were concerned, was the fact that this woman was a Samaritan and Jesus a Jew. Jews hated Samaritans, and the feeling was reciprocal.

Secondly, I love it because it's such an excellent example of Jesus' Semitic teaching style. It was a style that saw clear, concise, easily understood assertions as artless. In Semitic teaching you whet the appetite, you baffle, you lead your student on — to the point where the light suddenly dawns and he asserts the lesson himself. Almost as if he'd known it all along. The Greek philosopher, Plato, had some insight into this method as well.

Jesus whets the woman's appetite here. Perhaps, more accurately, He creates thirst. He does it artfully, by asking for a drink, as if He's the one who is thirsty. Then He leads the woman on, until finally He is able to say to her, in reference to the Messiah of Israel, "I who speak to you am He." It is marvelous!

Maybe one of the reasons I most love this story, though, is the woman's honesty. She had every reason to hide her marital status from Jesus, but didn't. She told it like it was, "I have no husband." I think this honesty was critical in the conversation. Jesus can speak to honest hearts. Expose your heart to Him, and He will expose His heart to you; hidden hearts, on the other hand, remain hidden.

This is why I chose verse 24 as the key verse. No question, we relate to God on the spiritual level, but our spirits are clouded as long as there is untruth in us. With God you've got to tell it like it is.

Prayer for Today: *We worship You today, Lord, in spirit and in truth, exposing the hidden recesses of our heart, that we may know Your heart and be drawn ever closer to You.*

Read John 5 *June 13*

Key Verse: John 5:46 "...*if you believed Moses, you would believe Me; for he wrote about Me."*

Can you trust someone who says he is God? Not likely. Maybe you heard the story of the pastor visiting a mental hospital. He walked by two of the patients sitting on a bench in the sunshine outside the main entrance.

"How ya doin', Reverend?" one of them asked brightly.

"Oh, quite fine, thank you" replied the pastor. "And what is your name, if I may ask?"

"Napoleon."

"Napoleon? *The* Napoleon?"

"Yep!", declared the man proudly.

"How do you know?" the pastor asked.

"God told me", he said.

"I did no such thing!" the other patient blurted.

One man thinks he's Napoleon; the other God. Little wonder these poor souls are being cared for in a hospital. It doesn't matter how sincere you are, or how convinced, the objective evidence doesn't line up with the subjective claim. So why should we believe Jesus when He says that He is God? The greatest objective evidence, I think, is the empty tomb. But Jesus himself said there were three other powerful objective evidences for His claim to deity. Here they are:

Firstly, "the very work that the Father has given Me to finish" (v.36). Secondly, "the Father who sent Me has Himself testified concerning Me." (v.37). And thirdly "The Scriptures — ...testify about me" (v.39). The work, the Father, the Scriptures. These are the three witnesses to Jesus.

His work included teaching, miracle working, and disciplining. The Father (*His* Father) declared both at Jesus' baptism and on the Mount of Transfiguration that He was His "beloved Son. Hear Him!" And the Scriptures, from Moses to the Prophets, speak clearly and unequivocally about Israel's Messiah who was to come. "I am He", says Jesus.

And who, in the light of the empty tomb, the post-resurrection appearances, the ascension and the profound, timeless impact of His work, can build a case against His claim? It's one thing to say He wasn't God. It's another thing to prove it.

Prayer for Today: *Dear Lord Jesus, we affirm in our heart today Peter's declaration, "You are the Christ, the Son of the living God" (Matthew 16:16).*

Read John 6 *June 14*

Key Verse: John 6:51c "...*the bread that I shall give is My flesh, which I shall give for the life of the world."*

Jesus certainly was skilled in alienating people. First of all there were His very exclusive claims to diety. Secondly, there was His flagrant disregard for the religious sensibilities of the Pharisees. Then there was His "lonerism"; He would get a big crowd, hanging on His every word, and thought nothing of walking (or boating, as the case may be) away. But the great offense was what is recorded in this chapter.

A day after Jesus had fed the five thousand with five barley loaves and two small fishes, He took the rest of the day off. That night He took a stroll on the lake — much to His disciples' astonishment. The next morning, some of the crowd from the day before caught up with Him in Capernaum. They wanted another free meal, but Jesus wouldn't co-operate. Then they asked for a sign — "How about some heavenly bread, Jesus?", they asked. Can you believe it? The food they had ingested at the previous day's miraculous meal wasn't even digested, and they're asking Jesus to perform "a miraculous sign" so they can believe in Him. Were they blind? Stupid? Or just plain dense?

Jesus ignores their lobotomous density and tells them (to continue the bread imagery) that He is, metaphorically, the "bread of life". Then comes the great offense.

He tells them they're going to have to "eat the flesh of the Son of Man and drink His blood" if they want to have "life". While they're gasping at that, He goes on to compare the bread of His flesh to the manna which their forefathers ate. Little wonder we read, "From this time many of His disciples turned back and no longer followed Him" (v.66). Jesus had gone too far. They had all heard or read enough of pagan religious systems which incorporated cannibalistic practices, and wanted nothing to do with this. "His ego has exploded", they must have thought. And Jesus just let them go, without any further explanation.

Little did any of His disciples realize that Jesus was speaking of His death on Calvary, where He became the "Lamb of God who takes away the sins of the world." The Passover seder's broken and blessed bread and the outpoured and blessed wine became the symbols of salvation. And every time we partake, we "remember His death, until He comes."

The great offense has become the great atonement.

Prayer for Today: *We pause now, beloved Lord, to remember Your broken body and spilled blood. Thank You for Your commitment to us, even unto death, and may we also exhibit such a total commitment to you.*

Read John 7 *June 15*

Key Verse: John 7:43 *"So there was division among the people because of Him."*

The setting for this chapter is Jerusalem during the Feast of Tabernacles. As you read it, you get a fascinating insight into the uproar surrounding Jesus in the public sector: He really rocked the boat.

For instance, He was an amazement to people simply in terms of His ability as a teacher — "How did this man get such learning without having studied?", they asked (v.15). Some were sure He was demon-possessed (v.20); others couldn't believe how immune He was to arrest, "Isn't this the man they are trying to kill? Here he is, speaking publicly, and they are not saying a word to him." So, some reasoned, maybe he is who he says he is, "Have the authorities really concluded that he is the Christ?" (vss. 25,26).

Then there were those who tried to figure out Jesus' teaching, but succeeded only in becoming more confused. "Where does this man intend to go, that we cannot find Him? Will he go where our people live scattered among the Greeks, and teach the Greeks? What does he mean when he said, 'You will look for me, but you will not find me,' and 'Where I am, you cannot come'?"

So some thought Jesus a prophet; others the Christ. Still others saw Him as a dangerous revolutionary, the sooner dead the better. But whatever your opinion of Jesus, you couldn't stay neutral anymore then than today — "the people were divided because of Jesus" (v.43).

Even the temple guards and the Pharisees were divided, and the Pharisees attributed any credence imputed to Jesus as nothing more than ignorance, "Has any of the rulers or of the Pharisees believed in him? No! But this mob that knows nothing of the law — there is a curse on them" (vss. 48,49).

There was only one clear voice in this "mob", only one clarion note in the chaos: the man Nicodemus. After his talk with Jesus by night, he had become a believer (albeit secret, at this point), and he was prepared to publicly give Jesus the benefit of the doubt (vss. 50,51).

Jesus still rocks the boat today. He is divisive. He's an either/or kind of person — there's no middle ground. you either accept Him or reject Him. He refuses to let us "halt between two opinions".

Prayer for Today: *Lord God, we pray that Jesus will be revealed to the whole world and please grant us the greatest opportunity human beings can ever have, the opportunity to be so filled with the Spirit of Christ that He is revealed through us.*

Read John 8 *June 16*

Key Verse: John 8:31 *"If you abide in My words, you are My disciples indeed."*

I like the way the NIV puts it, "If you hold to My teaching, you are really My disciples." The word "hold" is a strong verb; it speaks of mothers embracing their newborn, and ship-wrecked sailors clutching the life-line, refusing to let go. It speaks of commitment.

Whenever young couples come to me for premarital counselling, I tell them there are three words to remember in terms of making marriage last. Those words are, 1) commitment, 2) commitment, and 3) commitment. The marriage ceremony underscores the word — "...to have and to hold from this day forward. For better or for worse. In sickness and in health. For richer or for poorer. Till death us do part." That's the kind of foundation you can build a life on!

I've sometimes wondered if it might not be a bad idea for some of us evangelical pastors to make a bit more of a person's commitment to Christ at salvation than merely have them publicly "come forward". Why not put together a public ceremony wherein vows are expressed to Christ: where a new believer is gripped with the thrilling but awesome responsibility of what it means to call oneself a follower of Jesus, after he has made that initial "come forward" move.

The vows could go something like this: "I _____ take you now, Jesus Christ of Nazareth, as my Savior and Lord. I have acknowledged and confessed my sin; now I declare before this body of believers that my repentance has already begun. I turn away from my sin, and walk in a new direction. And, even as I do so, I charge this body with the responsibility of correcting and guiding me, as I grow from faith to faith. I am no longer my own. I belong to Christ even as I now take my place in His Body. I take hold of His teaching. I am His disciple. So help me God." Amen.

Prayer for Today: *Lord Jesus, we have confessed You openly before Your church in our water baptism and now we receive Jim's advice. Help us to confess Jesus afresh as we renew our membership in the local congregation.*

Read John 9 & 10   *June 17*

Key Verse: John 9:25b *"I was blind but now I see!"*

What a great story we read in chapter nine! Let me summarize it. Jesus is walking along and sees a man who was born blind. The disciples ask a question typical of orthodox religion of the time, "Who sinned, this man or his parents, that he was born blind?" Jesus answers, "Nobody sinned here." This offended the disciples' religious sensibilities, you can be sure!

He then goes through a little ritual of spit and mud and orders the blind man to find his way to the pool of Siloam. Onlookers must have felt some pity for this poor guy tottering down to the pool with his face disfigured by the mud. "Maybe he's gone off the deep end", some of them may have thought. But he did what Jesus commanded, and he "came home seeing", although he had yet to see his healer.

Then follows a series of discussions, interviews, and confrontations between the man and his religious superiors. The Pharisees (remember, they were the ancient equivalent of a lot of us orthodox evangelicals!) are so obtuse as to discredit the miracle because it happened on the Sabbath. The parents are brought into it, but they remain neutral, because they don't want to be thrown out of the synagogue over any Jesus Christ controversy. In the middle of it all is a man who had never seen but now sees. He's so stubborn in insisting on seeing and refusing to bad-mouth Jesus, that finally he is thrown out of the synagogue.

Then the man gets to meet his healer, face to face, eye to eye. At first he didn't recognize Jesus. How could he? But there must have been something about Jesus' voice or His touch. "Lord, I believe", the man says, and "worships" Jesus.

What was Jesus' assessment of it all? "For judgment I have come into this world, so that the blind will see and those who see will become blind" (v.39). Let's never think ourselves beyond need. If we do, we may find that our "guilt remains" (v.41).

Prayer for Today: Lord God, we are needy people. We need You for spirit, soul, mind and body. And today we say, "Lord we believe", and we worship You.

Read John 11   *June 18*

Key Verse: John 11:50 *"... it is expedient for you that one man should die for the people. ..."*

The raising of Lazarus from the dead was the final straw. The religious authorities were running scared. "If we let him go on like this...the Romans will come and take away our place (temple) and our nation", they cried (v.48). Especially threatened was the high priestly clique. As long as there was no messianic movement attracting the attention of Rome, the high priest and his "court" were virtually in charge of Jerusalem and the rich temple income, but any hint of political insurrection would end this comfortable situation. Jesus was now a political threat. He was a people mover and, indeed, a People Movement — a threat to the status quo. So Caiaphas, the high priest, decided the time to act had come. What he said was incitement to murder, but it seemed the only alternative. Jesus had to die.

"You do not realize", Caiaphas said to the Sanhedrin, "that it is better for you that one man die for the people than that the whole nation perish." John, the writer of this book, makes an editorial comment, "He did not say this on his own, but as high priest that year he prophesied that Jesus would die for the Jewish nation, and not only for that nation but also for the scattered children of God, to bring them together and make them one" (vss.51,52). Caiaphas was making an unconscious prophecy that Jesus would die for both Jew and Gentile. His incitement to murder was unknowingly a bold declaration of the purpose of God.

John would put it another way in another place, "For God so loved the world that He gave His only begotten Son, that whoever believes in Him should not perish but have everlasting life" (John 3:16).

Prayer for Today: *Lord God, our Father, thank You for using even Caiaphas to declare Your purpose. Now Lord, we ask that You'll use us today to declare Your purpose to others. We're willing and Your Word shows You're willing too. Therefore we expect it to happen today.*

Read John 12   June 19

Key Verse: John 12:43 "...*they loved the praise of men more than the praise of God.*"

The Sanhedrin was the ruling council of Jerusalem. They were Pharisees of high education, wealth and reputation who acted as judges, or rulers, over the Jewish people. Under the high priest, they acted as a sort of "Supreme Court", meeting from time to time as the situation warranted. In this chapter we read that "many even among the rulers believed" in Jesus. But they did so secretly, because their political survival depended on "the praise of men more than the praise of God."

Jesus warned these secret yet timorous believers, "When a man believes in Me, he does not believe in Me only, but in the One who sent Me. I have come into the world as a light, so that no one who believes in Me should stay in darkness. As for the person who hears My words but does not keep them, I do not judge him. For I did not come to judge the world, but to save it. There is a judge for the one who rejects Me and does not accept My words; that very word which I spoke will condemn him at the last day" (vss. 44-48 NIV). No doubt, Nicodemus and Joseph of Arimathea, both members of the Sanhedrin, were listening.

These two men must have gone through months of soul-searching. Like Christian politicians of today, they must have debated within themselves, or perhaps even together, as to whether they should outwardly vote with the party against their hearts in order to remain in a position to influence the system slowly and subtly, or whether they should openly declare their convictions and risk being voted out of power, thus nullifying their "salt and light" influence.

Nicodemus and Joseph finally decided to be "salt and light" outside of the political arenas. For it was they who, just a few days later, publicly identified with the crucified Christ — lovingly taking Him down from the cross, anointing His body for burial, and laying Him to rest in Joseph's own family sepulchre. They lost their earthly power, but gained a heavenly kingdom.

Prayer for Today: *O God, forgive us for any attitudes which love the praises of men more than Your commendation. By the working of Your Spirit and Your Word in us may we someday hear You say to us, "Well done."*

Read John 13 *June 20*

Key Verse: John 13:16 "*...a servant is not greater than his master...*"

I think most of us have the instinctive ability to discern between the merely obsequious and the purely altruistic. Huh? How's that again? What I mean is, we can usually tell when someone is being self-serving even while appearing to be serving us. And we can tell when someone is helping us purely for our sake, with no ulterior motive. In most cases, the altruistic person is ministering from a position of strength; not physical, mental, or financial strength, necessarily, but from moral strength. However shy, retiring, or self-effacing they may appear to be, there is a deep inner security characterizing their private world. They have moral fibre rooted in spiritual peace.

Notice the foundation of inner strength out of which Jesus ministered in this chapter — He "knew that the Father had put all things under His power, and that He had come from God and was returning to God..." (v.3). Jesus had nothing to prove and nothing to gain by washing His disciples' feet; but He *did* have a lesson to teach. Because He was their Master and Lord, His disciples would never be able to justify a superior attitude to the masses who would embrace Christianity over the succeeding centuries. Jesus had assumed the most lowly posture in washing His disciples' feet; for the remainder of the world's history, no Christian leader could afford to do less.

So we don't serve to get; we serve to give. Rather than striving, we rest in the confidence that we are loved. God has committed Himself to us, and He never backs down from what He has promised His children.

Prayer for Today: *Lord Jesus, You said that Your followers should wash one another's feet. Help me to serve someone today.*

Read John 14   *June 21*

Key Verse: John 14:2 *"I go to prepare a place for you."*

The death of a loved one always catches us off guard. We may have known for months that the tumour was malignant and our loved one was living with a six month sentence; but when the moment of death occurs, we're not as ready for it as we thought.

The next few days are a flurry of activity — phone calls to relatives and friends, visits to the undertaker, visits from those same relatives and friends, family meetings, and finally the funeral itself. After the interment, there's usually a social time, lots of tears, scores of pledges to keep in touch, "if there's anything I can do, don't hesitate to call", and then the crunch. Walking into that empty room; seeing those clothes still hanging in the closet; expecting to see him/her in their favorite chair. But the worst thing for many is seeing that empty place at the breakfast table. They're not there: they've left their place.

But, as far as God is concerned, they've *taken* their place. Our loss is heaven's gain. Jesus said, "I'm going to prepare a place for you."

"A place for you." Isn't that a wonderful thing! It affirms our individuality. It affirms God's providence. It affirms Jesus' power and purpose in and for our lives. It affirms hope.

Think back. So much of what you are today is the product of "places" you have occupied over the years. That bedroom. That tree-house. That cottage. That desk. Places that have imprinted you indelibly for a lifetime — positively and/or negatively.

What a joy to know there is one place none of us have seen yet; and it's the most important place of all. We will bear its imprint for eternity. And Jesus is the designer and builder!

It'll be a masterpiece!

Prayer for Today: *Lord God, may Your comforter, the Holy Spirit, enable us to comfort others with the Word of God. (1 Thessalonians 4:18; 5:11)*

Read John 15 & 16 *June 22*

Key Verse: John 15:7 *"If you abide in Me, and My words abide in you, you will ask what you desire, and it shall be done for you."*

I'm afraid a lot of us see God as a celestial errand-boy. He's there to do our will, meet our needs. And some of us have adopted various "get-what-you-want" systems. We think we know how to manipulate Him: all you need is to master the right praise system or prayer system and the magic button reveals itself — push and enjoy. And to add fuel to our fire, we quote half truths, or whole truths out of context. For instance, "...ask what you desire, and it shall be done for you." But we ignore the great qualifier.

"If you abide in Me, and My words abide in you...", *This* is the great qualifier. God is not giving us a carte blanche. Our will must conform with God's will or there is no deal. Our desire must spring out of His desire, and His desire is that we "bear much fruit", thereby glorifying the "Father" (v.8). Fruitfulness is the litmus test. God's glory is the chief end.

There are other qualifiers in this chapter. For instance, "You are My friends if you do what I command" (v.14). Or, "If you obey My commands, you will remain in My love..." (v.10). And what is Jesus' command? "My command is this: love each other as I have loved you" (v.12). The Lord isn't looking for religious people, or holy voters — He's looking for disciples — people who make Him glorious before the world.

I suppose the reminder that always bears repeating is this: we serve God, He doesn't serve us. He loves us with an everlasting love, and sent His Son to die for our sins, but He will never let us reduce Him to a means of achieving our own ends. In fact, when our faith becomes a way of getting our way, we've become heretics.

Jesus is Lord. He calls the shots.

Prayer for Today: *O Lord, You said in Your Word that it is only by the Holy Spirit that we can say (and mean it) that "Jesus is Lord". We invite Your Spirit to work mightily in us through the Word.*

Read John 17 & 18 *June 23*

Key Verse: John 17:26 *"I have made You known to them, and will continue to make You known..."*

Chapter 17 is known as Jesus' "High Priestly Prayer" for His disciples. It gives special insight into Jesus' assessment of His own ministry. It also helps us see what He expected of His Father in terms of the ongoing life of the church-to-be.

First, let's look at Jesus' self-assessment. What did He do? It shouldn't surprise us that the number one thing Jesus did was to make the Father glorious on earth. "I have brought You glory..." (v.4). How? By "completing the work You gave Me to do." In other words, by obedient action.

Then, Jesus revealed the Father "to those whom You gave Me" (v.6). To put it another way, Jesus uncovered God to the disciples (that's what "revelation" means: "to uncover"). In doing so, He "gave them the words You gave Me" (v.8). The uncovering was consistent with the Word of the Father. It was God's Word. This is what Jesus did and what Jesus was. He was God's Word even as He spoke God's words.

But Jesus also had expectations of His Father. He asks Him to protect them (vss. 11b,15). He asks Him to "sancitfy them by the truth..." (v.17) and to bring them "to complete unity" (v.23). He wants them to dwell in God (v.21).

Then Jesus makes a promise. He says He will "continue to make You [the Father] known "to the disciples (v.26). He will continue to uncover God so that the emerging Church will be drenched in an overflowing knowledge of God. Christianity will not be static, but dynamic: ever growing "from faith to faith" and in the "grace and knowledge of our Lord and Savior, Jesus Christ." This growth however, will be rooted in the solid soil of the Word of God. The living Word will always be the focus of the written word. The word will reveal the Word, and the Word will reveal the Father.

Prayer for Today: *Dear Heavenly Father, Your Son prayed for those who would believe in Him through the Word of the Apostles. That's us Lord. We open ourselves to You to truly answer Jesus' prayer in our lives.*

Read John 19 *June 24*

Key Verse: John 19:38b (NIV) *"Now Joseph was a disciple of Jesus, but secretly because he feared the Jews".*

After recording the events of the crucifixion and the touching scene around the foot of the cross, when Jesus entrusts His mother to John's keeping and care, John tells us about the burial. We might have expected the twelve disciples to come out of hiding, convicted in heart of their cowardice in deserting Jesus, and take the body down from the cross. Instead, we see two heretofore secret disciples, and the most unlikely candidates for the task.

Nicodemus and Joseph of Arimathea, both members of the Sanhedrin, and the two of all Jesus' disciples with the most to lose, courageously and lovingly declared their allegiance on that fateful day. They were secret believers. Nicodemus was the one who had come to see Jesus under the cover of night, and one wonders if Joseph had not had a similar nocturnal interchange with Jesus. Somehow they had connected, for obviously they had planned, however quickly, what they should do about the burial. They had also counted the cost. Their positions with the Sanhedrin were forfeit if they identified publicly with the crucified Christ. Their influence, status, and even most of their long-term friendships were shot. They were about to enter a social wasteland.

They worked hurriedly, for the Sabbath was almost upon them. As the sun sank into the western sky, they took Christ's body down from the cross, suffering ritual defilement as they touched the dead flesh. They wrapped Him in strips of cloth, packing between each layer the burial spices Nicodemus had brought. Then, with their own hands, they carried their Master to Joseph's own grave. Gently and sorrowfully, they laid Him there. As the sun disappeared, it seemed all hope disappeared with it. The two grieving brothers slowly walked away.

Nicodemus and Joseph were outstanding men in terms of their public profile, but were retiring in their faith. They "feared the Jews". Like you and me they shied away from the cost of discipleship; at least, they had done so most of the time. But now they acted differently, when it was toughest. It is no great matter, declared Cardinal Newman, that we obey the Master in the ninety and nine cases where to do so is easy. The real test for us lies in the hundredth case, where it is hard.

Jesus, our Saviour and Lord, is able to empower us to do what we never thought possible. Nicodemus and Joseph know all about that.

Prayer For Today: *Father God, as Pilate said to the crowd, "Behold the man," he directed the gaze of all history to Your Son and our Saviour, Jesus. Grant that we may ever focus our gaze upon Him who alone is the Author and Finisher of our faith.*

Read John 20 & 21 *June 25*

Key Verse: John 20:28 *"And Thomas answered and said to Him, 'My Lord and my God!'"*

Arthur John Gossip writes, "That night that Christ came, Thomas had not been present. We do not know why. But is there not here a warning for us not to forsake the assembling of ourselves together? How much many miss, who make only an occasional, spasmodic, irregular appearance at the worship of God in his house! 'For where two or three are gathered together in my name, there am I in the midst of them', so Christ promises (Mt. 18:20). And sometimes surely had they been there, to them, too, He would have appeared!" (Interpreters Bible, Vol. 8, p. 798).

John has already presented Thomas to us as fatalistically daring (11:16) and bluntly skeptical (14:5). He was pragmatic and honest. He wasn't about to be caught up in the hysteria and the unreal imaginings of a distraught and devastated group of cloistered disciples. Yes, he was disappointed, bitterly so, just like the rest of them. But he was not going to be party to a delusive reconstruction of Jesus. He was dead, period. So let's accept that and get real. The sooner we can get on with life, the better.

Frankly, I identify with Thomas. He cherished the truth.

And the Truth cherished him. A week later, Jesus made a gracious concession to Thomas' skepticism. "Put your finger here, and see My hands; and put out your hand, and place in it My side; do not be faithless, but believing" (20:27). Thomas' response is the response of the Church, "My Lord and my God!"

Church history tells us Thomas was the one disciple who travelled the farthest to a martyr's grave. In so doing, he brought the message of the risen Saviour to the sub-continent of India. Thank God for Thomas!

Prayer for Today: *"My Lord and my God", we confess with Thomas the truth of who You are Lord Jesus. Grant to us now the blessing of being living proofs of the reality of that statement in our lives.*

Introduction to
The Book of Deuteronomy

Deuteronomy is the last book of the Pentateuch. It completes the five books of Moses, a literary unit called the *Torah*, or "The Law". The Hebrew title for Deuteronomy is taken from the first words of the book, *elleh haddebarim*, meaning "these are the words", or it is often more simply referred to as *debarim*, "words". The English title "Deuteronomy" came from the Greek and Latin translations of the book, meaning "second law". Indeed, much of the book reviews the Law God gave at Sinai, but it also expounds and adapts this original Law to make it applicable to the new generation to whom this book is addressed.

Moses must have felt it necessary after the rebellious generation had perished, and before his imminent death, to distinctly present these important laws to the new generation who had not been present at Sinai when God gave the Law. This was done to prepare the people spiritually before they entered the Promised Land. The whole purpose of the book was to see them renew their covenant relationship with God.

Moses spoke these words to the people in the form of a warm, heartfelt exhortation. His words were also written down for future generations, and there are more than eighty references to Deuteronomy in the New Testament. Jesus and His apostles often quoted from this book. Peter quoted a prophecy concerning the coming of Jesus Christ from Deuteronomy 18:15-19, as did Stephen (Acts 3:22-23; 7:37).

Moses encouraged the Israelites to obey God's laws that they might receive His blessings and enjoy the privileges of the covenant. He warned that disobedience would result in divine punishments. Moses attempted to spiritually awaken them that they might understand more fully the significance of their covenant relationship with God and the obligations involved, and that they might love Him with all their heart, soul and mind, for as Moses clearly expressed in his sermons, God first loved them.

Read Deuteronomy 1 *June 26*

Key Verse: Deuteronomy 1:39 *"Your little ones and your children, who you say will be victims,...they shall go in there; to them I will give it, and they shall possess it."*

Moses was addressing these same "little ones" whom their parents feared would be victims. They were now adults and on the verge of possessing the very land their fathers had spurned. Moses taught them about the past that they might learn from the mistakes of their parents, gain knowledge of the covenant that had been broken, and learn more of their God. Although they were now physically ready to enter the land, they had yet to become spiritually ready. Moses' speech was important for the people to take to heart, for if it failed they might once again be rejected from entering the Promised Land.

Moses began from the beginning of their journey from the mountain range of Horeb, of which Sinai is one peak (the area where the law had been given and the covenant ratified), on their way to possess their God-given land. He mentions that it is an eleven-day journey from Horeb to Kadesh Barnea (1:2), and from there they were to enter the land that God had given them as a possession; all they had to do was take it as one would receive a gift, but because of rebellion against God, their short journey turned into a thirty-eight year ordeal.

In the final few months before his death, Moses was concerned that his people learn lasting things of significance from him. He wanted to be sure they would respect those whom God had put in authority over them, like Joshua (1:38) and the judges. He confirmed their judicial office in recalling the wise advice of his father-in-law, and he acted upon it in appointing them to help him bear the burden of all the people (Exodus 18:17-21,24). This served as a reminder that it was really God who was their judge and sovereign, so they were to always promote righteous administration of justice to all. In recalling this same instance, Moses showed God's faithfulness in keeping His promise to Abraham about multiplying his seed (1:10; Genesis 12:2; 15:5). He thus encouraged the new generation to step out in faith and take possession of Canaan, for in this, too, God would keep His promise.

Moses revealed how God had guided and carried Israel as a loving parent to the land He was giving them. God would go before them, fight for them and give them the victory. Yet, in faithless fear, they had requested spies to first enter the land (1:22). This led to discouragement, complaining, rebellion, God's anger, and their punishment. How could they have been so ungrateful as to say, "Because the Lord hates us", especially when the opposite was so evident? Would the merciful God deliver them from bondage in Egypt to only see their death at the hands of the Amorites (1:27)? Moses wanted this younger generation to see that this was impossible and he challenged their faith. In fact, their standing before Moses was in itself a testimony of God's goodness. In their parents' rebellion and breach of the covenant, they had complained to God that their little ones would be victims, but here they all were, listening to Moses and learning of God's covenant faithfulness.

Moses taught them of God's grace and goodness, and it was illustrated by His renewing the covenant with them, even though they had been rebellious. Moses showed them that disobedience and rebellion against God can only bring disaster. This was evident in yet their second rebellion of going to fight without the Lord being with them (1:42-44; Numbers 14:42-45). Israel was to learn that God's presence was essential for victory, just as it is for victory in our lives today.

Their parents' disbelief brought God's judgment upon them in being excluded from entering their beautiful land and in dying in the wilderness. However, even in His judgment, God still showed mercy, for not only the godly men, Caleb and Joshua, would be allowed to enter, but also the whole second generation of Israel (1:39). This promise to grant a gracious new beginning was now being fulfilled, for the purpose of God cannot be stopped.

Prayer for today: *Lord God, You are the God of new beginnings. Grant that our children and our children's children, should You tarry in Your glorious return, will rise up to follow You more fully than we have.*

Read Deuteronomy 2 *June 27*

Key Verse: Deuteronomy 2:7 *"For the Lord your God has blessed you in all the work of your hand. He knows your trudging through the great wilderness. These forty years the Lord your God has been with you; you have lacked nothing."*

In this chapter, Moses continued teaching the new generation of their history, bringing it up to their own time and events in which they were involved. He laid stress on the fact that even while Israel was exiled to the hard life of the wilderness, God continued to guide and care for them. They were in a period of discipline, but not abandonment. Though they had rejected God and insulted Him by their words and rebellion, He lovingly saw to it that they lacked nothing (2:7). They had sufficient food, water, clothing and divine protection.

It appears that most of their wanderings were in the area of Mount Seir until the Lord gave them word to go northward (2:1-3). They had a specific destination; they were not to wage war, nor take the territory of their "brethren" from Edom (descendants of Esau), Moab, or Ammon (descendants of Lot), for they were kinsmen, and God had given them their lands as a possession. God had also driven out and destroyed the "giants" (men of large stature) for these descendants of Abraham. Hearing this would encourage the new generation of Israelites, for if God had done this for those people, He surely would do the same for His own chosen people. Therefore, they were not to fear the large people in the land of Canaan as their parents had done. Learning of this would give them courage and confidence to boldly go in and take the land of Canaan.

By the time they crossed over the Valley of Zered (the main valley and stream from the east which flows into the southern end of the Dead Sea), all the fighting men who had been numbered in the first census and who had rebelled against God (Numbers 1; 14:29) had died, just as the Lord had said. From this time on, God began to move in a mighty way and caused the other nations to fear Israel (2:25), for His army was on the move. He announced to all the new generation of fighting men: "Rise, take your journey" (2:24). Because the Lord was with them, they went on to be victorious over Sihon, king of the Amorites, and to possess his land (cf. Numbers 21:21-24). Their time was indeed ripe for judgment, as the Lord had prophesied to Abraham, and it came about at the set time of Israel's conquest (cf. Genesis 15:16). There were still Amorites in the land of Canaan who had yet to be conquered, but all those who had spread into Transjordan were totally destroyed. With this victory, God demonstrated His power and absolute authority on behalf of Israel.

This story of victory told to them by Moses would give courage and faith to go on believing that God would again go before them and give them more victories, for they had yet to cross the Jordan and engage in battle with the Canaanites. However, knowing their enemies feared them and that God would be with them must have given them tremendous confidence, not in themselves, but in God who would enable them by His power. God was, and still is, in control of events and gives victory and blessings to those who are faithful and obedient to Him.

Prayer for today: *O Lord, we thank You for the great blessings upon us in the past. May our present and future be blessed, too. Please guide, protect and inspire us to follow in Your perfect plan.*

Read Deuteronomy 3 June 28

Key Verse: Deuteronomy 3:22 *"You must not fear them, for the Lord your God Himself fights for you."*

After defeating Sihon, the Amorite king of Heshbon (2:32-33), Israel advanced toward the Jordan River in the area of Bashan where Og, king of Bashan, came out against Israel with defiance and force. God had already warned Israel of this conflict; He had encouraged Israel not to fear and promised to do the same with Og as he had done to Sihon (3:1-2). The Lord was faithful in delivering them into Israel's hands (3:6; cf. Numbers 21:33-35). Even though Og was a huge and mighty warrior, he was not to be feared. No man's power can secure him against the power of the Almighty. Moses mentioned Og's great "iron bed" to illustrate that though he was indeed a giant (probably twice the height of an average man), the Lord had given Israel a great victory over him, and therefore there was no need to fear those large people in the land of Canaan as had their parents (cf. Numbers 13:28).

Moses also reminded Israel that Og (as well as Sihon; 2:36) had many large fortified cities with "high walls, gates, and bars", but they, as well as all the inhabitants, were "utterly destroyed" (3:5-6). With these words, Moses encouraged and challenged the new armed forces to go forth boldly into Canaan and conquer the giants and their cities just as God had done for them before.

With the fall of Sihon and Og, the vast territory on the east side of the Jordan River came into the hands of Israel. These victories were later often mentioned together to the praise of God, because with them Israel's other triumphs began (e.g. Psalm 135:10-12). This newly conquered territory would give Israel great encouragement and would also give Moses a taste of the coming victories that he himself would not see. Moses was also able to see the tribes of Reuben, Gad, and the half tribe of Manasseh receive their inheritance of land. However, this was conditional upon their support in continuing to fight and see all the other tribes receive their "rest" and inheritance as well (3:18-20; Numbers 32:18). Moses used this opportunity to remind these tribes of this, their obligation.

God gave Moses a foretaste of the future before his death by seeing some receive their inheritance, and by seeing the Lord victorious in battle. Yet this was not sufficient; Moses strongly desired to enter the Promised Land himself to see more victories yet to come; this was his prayer. God was angered by Moses' request and refused him entrance, but would permit him to see the land from a distance. God's solemn word does not change, as Moses should have known (Numbers 20:12; 27:14). It seems that Moses did not realize he would indeed soon see the manifestations of God and His glory in an even better way in the life hereafter than in remaining physically alive to enter Canaan. His exclusion would also serve as a lesson for all the people that there is a price to pay for disobedience to God.

Moses' final duties, besides the covenant renewal ceremony (29:10-15), were to challenge the people not to fear, but to conquer, for "God Himself fights for you" (3:22). He would also commission and encourage Joshua to lead them in the conquest (3:21, 28; Numbers 27:18-23). Joshua may have been reluctant to take such a great responsibility, so Moses was to encourage him and give him support. Joshua was also assured that he was God's choice and that God would fight for him. When God chooses someone for His work, He sends others to encourage and give support. Most importantly, He Himself will give the greatest support.

For those believers who are close to passing on into glory, it must be a comfort to know that the Lord will see that their work in furthering His kingdom is carried on, just as it must have been a comfort for Moses. Although he was not allowed to march into Canaan, Moses must have been satisfied that God's will and purpose would still be accomplished. The torch was now to be passed on to another: his task had been accomplished.

Prayer for today: *O Lord, grant us a more perfect love for You, for Your Word declares, "Perfect love casts out fear." Thus, emboldened by our love for You, we will march forward in Your plan for our lives until that time when, by Your grace, we hear You say, "Well done."*

Read Deuteronomy 4   *June 29*

Key Verse: Deuteronomy 4:7 *"For what great nation is there that has God so near to it, as the Lord our God is to us, for whatever reason we may call upon Him?"*

Moses' historical review closes with this wonderful chapter of exhortation. The emphasis throughout is for Israel to serve God in obedience. Several reasons are given that warrant this obedience to their sovereign God, providing a necessary prelude to the laws He would soon declare in confirming the covenant. Before the close of the chapter, Moses himself was an example of obedience to God by setting up the three cities of refuge in Transjordan as the Lord had commanded (4:41-43; Numbers 35:14).

Moses based his appeal for obedience upon the greatness of God and His mighty deeds on their behalf, especially in graciously delivering them from bondage in Egypt and in speaking the Commandments to them from within the fire on Sinai, thus making a covenant with them because of His love for their fathers, the patriarchs, especially for Abraham. All this had been shown to Israel that they "might know that the Lord Himself is God; there is none other besides Him"·(4:35). A second appeal for obedience was based on the perfection of His Law, for it was clearly evident that no other nation had a divinely given code (4:8). Most importantly, the appeal was made because their God was indeed true and present among them; He was accessible (4:7). No other god was like this, for the gods of other nations were false. Only the God of Israel could hear and answer prayer, for He dwelt among His people (cf. Psalm 46:1,5). What a privileged people the Israelites were, and what a privileged people we are today to be in the new covenant with God through His Son Jesus Christ.

The Israelites were to be motivated to keep the laws of God when they entered the land and settled. They were to know that these laws were not just for that period of time, but for all their generations to come. Therefore, they were warned to be careful not to forget, nor change the law, but to pass it on in its original form to their children and grandchildren (4:9). This shows the importance of parents teaching their children the Word of God within the home. Nothing can replace these special times within the family.

We see in this chapter several different motives offered for obedience to God's Law, both positively and negatively: Positively, obedience leads to life, a rich inheritance, wisdom, closeness with God, enjoyment of the blessings of the covenant, and knowledge of righteousness. Negatively, disobedience leads to death, destruction, God's wrath and judgment.

Moses prophesied in this discourse to God's chosen people that they would fall into the sin of idolatry. He repeatedly warned them concerning this evil. He explained that when they heard God's voice from the midst of the fire, they saw no form, so neither were they to make any carved images to which they would bow down (4:15-16; cf. Ex. 20:4,5; John 1:18; 4:24). Yet later in their history, Israel did this very thing, provoking God's wrath and leading to their national destruction and exile (4:25-28). However, Moses explained that their God was compassionate and merciful, never forgetting His covenant and promise to Abraham. He foretold that while in exile, "you will seek the Lord your God, and you will find Him if you seek Him with all your heart and with all your soul" (4:29). Because of this, God would renew His covenant with them and bring restoration. He would hear their desperate prayers, even in a distant, heathen land. Here we see expounded the graciousness and love of God.

Prayer for today: Lord, thank You for Your Word to our generation. Please give us the necessary dedication as parents, grandparents, uncles, aunts and neighbours to pass on Your Word to future generations.

Read Deuteronomy 5 & 6   *June 30*

Key Verse: Deuteronomy 6:5 *"You shall love the Lord your God with all your heart, with all your soul, and with all your might."*

Before entering the Promised Land, it was necessary that this new generation of Israelites realize the signficance of their covenant with God. Therefore, Moses relates some specific details of the covenant made at Mount Horeb (Sinai) forty years previously. He emphasized that the Ten Commandments were still relevant to them (just as they are still relevant to us today). Based on God's redemptive act of delivering Israel from Egypt (for which they are indebted to Him), Moses challenged them to live in consecration and obedience to God, their sole Sovereign. This is a stipulation of the covenant which they were in the process of renewing and solemnizing.

Moses repeated the Ten Commandments to the new generation with some slight variations, considering the present situation of Israel as they were in preparation for entering the Promised Land (cf. Exodus 20:3-17). These ten basic laws established the foundation of Israel's relationship with God. They had a great impact on Israel's history, as well as on the world today, since they are the foundation for moral principles and modern law. If Israel would be careful to observe these commands of God and walk in His ways, the blessings of the covenant would result (5:33; 6:2-3). However, curses would result for breaking them (28:15ff).

To serve as an example for the people, Moses told them of their parents' response in hearing these Ten Commandments with God's own audible voice from the burning mount; it brought a godly fear and reverence for the Lord their God. This great manifestation (5:22) showed God's redemptive grace toward sinful man, that He would reveal to them even this limited degree of His glory. However, they feared for their lives, for in experiencing the holiness of God so closely, they felt all the more their own sinfulness and unworthiness. Therefore, they pleaded that Moses would from then on serve as their mediator. God's response showed His great love for them (and their descendants).

He yearned that they would always fear Him and keep His commands, "that it might be well with them and with their children forever!" (5:29). The Lord desired to bless His people, just as He desires to do so for His children today.

Moses' challenge to obedience is greatly elaborated on in chapter six. He stressed the oneness of God in the famous verse known as the shema , (Hebrew for "hear", the first word of the verse, 6:4). This divinely revealed insight concerning their God, *Yahweh*, was a strong declaration of monotheism (belief in one God) against the common belief of their day in polytheism (many gods). The Israelites were to serve and worship Him alone, for only the God of Israel was, and is, a true deity. Moses, knowing the coming danger and temptations for Israel in the land of Canaan, strongly warned them to "not go after other gods", for He is "a jealous God" (6:14-15), and His wrath would be the result. How then were they to remember their God when they are settled and comfortable in Canaan? Moses gave a concise answer: "[1] fear the Lord your God...[2] serve Him, and...[3] take oaths in His name" (6:13). The third way seems to mean a continual renewal of the oath of allegiance to God in a life dedicated to Him.

Moses gave practical illustrations of how they were to fear and serve God when in the land. They were to internalize God's laws that they might be reflected in every aspect of life; in their thinking and conversation with others, as well as through outward means (6:9). It was also very important to teach their children the laws of God and to bring Him glory in relating the story of their redemptive history (6:7, 20-23). Most importantly, they were to love the Lord their God with all their being, which would naturally result in reverent obedience to all His commandments and walking in His ways (6:5; cf. 11:1,22; John 14:15). Jesus Christ called this "the first and great commandment" (Matthew 22:38).

Prayer for today: *Lord, as we prayed yesterday for Your grace to pass on Your Word, today we pray for ourselves, that we will be truly separated unto You in holiness of conduct so that our life-styles will confirm the truth of our words to the next generations.*

Proclaiming the
Good News of Jesus
— Since 1962 —

THE CROSSROADS CHRISTIAN COMMUNICATIONS FAMILY OF MINISTRIES:

100 HUNTLEY STREET: Daily Christian television since 1977. Viewers obtain counselling and prayer through dozens of telephone counselling centres.

CIRCLE SQUARE: Top quality Christian programming for children. This fast-paced weekly show is popular in many countries around the world.

CIRCLE SQUARE RANCHES: Started as a follow-up to the Circle Square program, there are now nine ranches offering summer camping programs for children and year-round retreats.

CMP: Christian Missions Productions has produced Christian programs in 17 languages other than English.

NITE LITE: Late night live open-line television in which the host matches real problems of callers with the answers of the Gospel.

HEART TO HEART FAMILY MINISTRIES: Marriage and family counselling and seminars promoting Biblical wholeness in the home.

KINGDOM ADVENTURE: State-of-the-art children's programming combining puppetry and animation to teach Biblical truths and values.

CHRISTIAN BROADCAST ACADEMY: Television production training for men and women of vision who want this medium used for the Gospel.

DAVID MAINSE CRUSADES: Interdenominational, area-wide evangelistic crusades.

E.R.D.F.: The Emergency Response and Development Fund: For years, TV viewers have responded whenever stories of human need have been featured.

If you would like information on becoming a partner with us through your prayerful and financial support, please write your request to: C.C.C.I., 100 Huntley Street, Toronto, Ontario, Canada M4Y 2L1.

Notes

Notes

Notes

Notes

Notes